W9-ANN-107

The Asia Crisis

The Asia Crisis

The Cures, their Effectiveness and the Prospects After

Edited by

Tran Van Hoa
Associate Professor
University of Wollongong
Australia

First published in Great Britain 2000 by
MACMILLAN PRESS LTD
Houndmills, Basingstoke, Hampshire RG21 6XS and London
Companies and representatives throughout the world

A catalogue record for this book is available from the British Library.

ISBN 0–333–75389–5

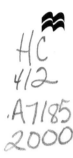

First published in the United States of America 2000 by
ST. MARTIN'S PRESS, INC.,
Scholarly and Reference Division,
175 Fifth Avenue, New York, N.Y. 10010

ISBN 0–312–22589–X

Library of Congress Cataloging-in-Publication Data
The Asia crisis : the cures, their effectiveness and the prospects
after / edited by Tran Van Hoa.
p.   cm.
Includes bibliographical references and index.
ISBN 0–312–22589–X
1. Financial crises—Asia.   2. Economic forecasting—Asia.
3. Asia—Economic conditions—1945–   4. Asia—Commerce.   I. Tran,
Van Hoa.
HC412.A7185   1999
332'.095—dc21   99–15306
                                                                        CIP

This book is printed on paper suitable for recycling and made from fully managed and sustained
forest sources.

10   9   8   7   6   5   4   3   2   1
09   08   07   06   05   04   03   02   01   00

Printed and bound in Great Britain by
Antony Rowe Ltd, Chippenham, Wiltshire

To the fond memory of Aida

Contents

List of Tables and Figures

Tables

Figures

Acknowledgements

The Asian economic and financial crisis has brought about untold economic and social damages and political instability to the countries in trouble (Thailand, Indonesia, Korea, Malaysia, and the Philippines) and, to a lesser extent, to other Asian economies (e.g. Hong Kong, China and Singapore). The book is the second in a series of books we plan to publish on this crisis and has three objectives.

First, it is to provide a better and deeper understanding of the crisis and, as a result, to help relevant governments or organizations formulate more appropriate national and international cures or remedies. Secondly, the book provides an authoritative and comprehensive assessment by international experts on the various rescue packages and reform plans proposed by either the innternational organizations such as the International Monetary Fund, the World Bank and the Asian Development Bank or national governments, and critically examines their effectiveness to draw useful positive or negative lessons in the area for the future. Finally, the book provides a vision for international development of growth, trade, investment and business in the short and long terms. This vision is based on a serious and comprehensive analysis of current issues and problems, projections from official government reform plans and the contributors' own calculations and forecasts. The prospects for Asian and world economies are then presented qualitatively or quantitatively in a concise and integrated manner in a number of chapters of the book for use in informed discussions, strategic planning or in policy analysis by governments, businesses, institutions, academics, students and all other interested people.

The editor is indebted to Tim Farmiloe of Macmillan for his encouragement in the preparation of the book. He is also indebted to his colleagues and friends from the various government departments, the business community, research institutes and universities in Australia and overseas for generously giving their support and advice to the project. Last but not least, the editor would like to thank all his contributors for their quick responses to the initiative to publish this book and their marvellous cooperation and contribution to an area of contemporary national and international significance with widespread economic, social and political interest.

Wollongong   TRAN VAN HOA
October 1998

Notes on the Contributors

Apichai Puntasen is Professor of Economics, Thammasat University, Thailand.

Charles Harvie is Associate Professor, Department of Economics, University of Wollongong, Australia.

Frank Hiep Huynh was formerly Senior Lecturer, School of Business, La Trobe University, Australia.

Li Jingping is an economist in the Department of Statistics and Economics, the Renmin University of China, Beijing, China.

Kitti Limskul is Associate Professor and Director of the Economic Modelling and Forecasting Program, Chulalongkorn University, Thailand.

Tran Van Hoa is Associate Professor, University of Wollongong, Australia.

Zhao Yanyun is Professor of Economics and Chairman of the Department of Statistics and Economics, the Renmin University of China, Beijing, and an Advisor to the Central Government, China.

Part I

1

The Asian Crisis and World Prospects: An Overview

Tran Van Hoa

1. Introduction

The Asian economic and financial crisis started in July 1997 in Thailand and spread quickly to other East Asian economies with devastating effects, economically, financially, socially and politically. Strong economies in Asia such as Hong Kong, Taiwan, Singapore, China and Japan have also been affected by the contagion of this major turmoil. Far away countries in Eastern Europe (e.g., Russia) and in Latin and North Americas (e.g., Argentina, Brazil and the US) and Western Europe (e.g., Germany) all have experienced the damages the Asian meltdown has generated. The crisis is a contemporary global issue in the days of economic and financial globalization, worldwide digital telephony and electronic commerce. Being a global issue, the impact and resulting damages of the crisis have also taken on an international nature concerning directly or indirectly such essential issues as development, growth, employment, unemployment, investment, trade, business, education, industry, tourism, politics, government and social welfare in all sectors of the affected countries. Rescue packages and reform plans have been proposed and adopted as a result of tenuous negotiations between national governments and international organizations such as the International Monetary Fund (IMF), the World Bank (WB), the Asian Development Bank (ADB) and many other relevant institutions.

Unfortunately for the people of the affected countries and also, although to a lesser extent, for the remedy proponents, many of these rescue packages and reform plans have, because of their hastily constructed nature or inappropriately diagnosed and prescribed remedies, proved to be ineffective in most economies in trouble. In the meantime, the ravages of the Asian slowdown continue marching on relentlessly, bringing untold economic hardships even and especially to the grass-roots level of the population in the countries in crisis, and in a number of them social unrest national division and fatalities in a number of them. Numerous World Economic Summit conferences and Asia Pacific Economic Cooperation (APEC) Forum meetings have taken place to discuss the crisis-based problems and how to solve them effectively and quickly, but it seems that the world as a whole (including politicians, economists, financial analysts, business people, corporate planners, academics and other experts) has not been able to pinpoint accurately and substantively the fundamental causes of this major economic turmoil of our times and to provide appropriate cures for it. What are the prospects, if any, for Asian and world economies under this situation in the short and long term?

2.   The issues and prospects from the crisis

The present book attempts to provide an answer to this important question which is useful to international cooperation, government planning, corporate forward strategies, commerce and industry studies, and formal and informal academic investigations. The book is in its essence a soundly researched, data-based, well-interpreted and well articulated analysis of the prospects for Asian and world economies well into the twenty-first century, from which future theoretical, applied and policy analyses in economics, finance, industry and commerce can bring meaningful knowledge to better decision making, and experience in data analysis and methodological exposure to practical policy problems. The specific areas of research, interpretation and reportage of the findings covered in the book can be summarized as follows:

A concise analysis of the prospects for Asian and world economies is prepared for Chapter 2 by Tran Van Hoa. In this chapter, the writer discusses the various aspects or perspectives of the pertinent issues (ie, causes and remedies) of the Asian crisis and their effectiveness (or the lack of it) so far in the affected countries. World economy reforms as proposed by major national economies (such as Japan) and international organizations (such as the IMF), their likely successes in implementation and their prospects in general are also critically evaluated.

In Chapter 3, Kitti Limskul of Chulalongkorn University gives a detailed analysis of the financial and economic (or balance of payment) turmoil in Thailand, starting from the deregulation of the financial market in the early 1990s and the policy mistakes made by financial authorities there during the early days. The widespread social impact of the turmoil in the country is investigated and the various government plans and programmes to minimize it in the years to come are also assessed.

Chapter 4, written by Apichai Puntasen of Thammasat University, draws on his decade-long experience in the self-help village programmes and in rural development in Thailand to provide a fresh approach to solving the crisis in the country: the use of Buddhist economics. This kind of economics contrasts itself to Western mainstream economics in the adoption of an individual or social objective function to be optimized under appropriate constraints and for a clement or friendly environment in the tropical region of the world. The constraints are based on a Buddhist view of the human being and the interpretation of its existence and, like some centuries-old precepts from the Middle East, question the goodness of capital accumulation and profit-seeking (including by speculation) in the free-wheeling world financial market.

Concise comments on the use of Buddhist economics or Asian and nationalistic Japanese-style economic systems are given by Tran Van Hoa in Chapter 5 in which he elucidates further the difference and similarity between the objectives, methodologies and applications of Buddhist and Western economics. The elucidation covers the main aspects of consumption (and production) in modern economic theory and the basic tenets of Buddhist and Asian economics, their axioms and theorems, and their practical applications. The relevance of the discussion is carried out in the light of contemporary developments such as the internationalization of trade, investment and business, and economic and financial globalization.

Chapter 6 written by Tran Van Hoa deals with Japan's current economic and financial problems which many believe are leading the country and many other countries trading with it to a new economic crisis with far reaching economic and social effects on the world economies. The chapter points out the importance of trade in the history of the Japanese economy, Japan's economic and political position in the world, the problems with its banking and financial institutions and operations and reform and restructuring plans by its Economic Council to avoid a national and international economic crisis. Japan's economy and reform plans are also assessed in the light of the emergence of economic globalization and borderless electronic commerce.

Charles Harvie discusses and evaluates in Chapter 7 the current issues in Indonesia 16 months after the crisis took place there and after the operation of the new government under President Habibie. He also looks at the conditions for a quick and stable recovery of the Indonesian economy from the path of economic and social collapse experienced some months ago. His prognosis on the economic future of Indonesia gives serious thought to some challenging issues facing this economy in the next few years.

The case of Malaysia is analysed in Chapter 8 by Frank Hiep Huynh of La Trobe University. In this chapter, he first surveys the current issues and problems in the Malaysian economy and the road the country has taken under the forceful direction of its often outspoken prime minister to preserve the country's policy of independence. His analysis seems to indicate that the cures for Malaysia as developed by the country itself have the tendency of isolating the evil forces of economic globalization but, in many important aspects, they are very similar to those rescue remedies suggested by the IMF. The prospects for Malaysia are nevertheless good as judged by both internal and international experts.

In Chapter 9, Zhao Yanyun and Li Jingping of the People's University of China deal with the issues of foreign trade in the transition economies in general and in China in particular. To them, the issue of competitiveness in trade is important for understanding the fundamental cause of the Asian economic crisis. It is this competitiveness (or the lack of it) that has given rise to the problems (unnoticed by many experts and authorities) many years before the turmoil did occur in Thailand in July 1997. An assessment of other economies in the light of this fresh new approach using international competitiveness is also given.

Again in Chapter 10, Charles Harvie reports his recent findings for China and poses the question most people seem to want to ask and to have a definitive answer for: Will China become the next piece of the economic domino in East Asia? His analysis seems to indicate the complexity of the issue and emphasizes the important role played by other Asian economies (including Japan) in affecting the future direction of China's economic development and policy.

In summary, the book gives a good coverage of contemporary issues and problems of both national and international significance facing the Asian economies, including the economies that have not seriously been affected by the Asian economic crisis of 1997 as well as other countries in other regions of the world which started at the end of 1998 to be influenced by this serious turmoil. Based on current data and analysis, the conclusions that have been advanced by the contributors to the book for possible use in policy formulation and implementation or for further studies seem to indicate the severity, complexity and deep impact of the Asian meltdown and the not so easy solution for it. While it can be assumed that the real causes of growth and development and, unfortunately, also the Asian crisis are related to foreign trade and the characteristics of its competitiveness in an environment of economic globalization and electronic money, the prospects for Asian and world economies depend crucially on the interaction of future developments and trends in all these issues.

At the time of writing, these prospects are not promising at least in the short term. This conclusion can be used to indicate the seriousness of the crisis and its contagion and the need for better remedies for it. An international effort with collective consensus and without narrow national or regional interest may help find the solution more effectively.

2
The Asia Crisis and Prospects After

Tran Van Hoa

1. Introduction

Some time has elapsed since the Asia financial or economic crisis first emerged in July 1997 in Thailand. During that time, we have witnessed the severe economic, political and social damages caused by the meltdown (characterized by a stunt growth and even a recession arising from huge and sudden currency devaluation and heavy falls in the stock market) in the once miracle economies in the Asian region. We have also witnessed the subsequent contagion of the crisis in Thailand to important Asian economies such as Indonesia, Korea, Malaysia and the Philippines. Other economically strong countries in Asia, such as Hong Kong, Singapore, Taiwan, China and Japan, and countries beyond Asia, for example, Russia, the Subcontinent, Latin America (Argentina and Brazil), North America and Europe, all have been to a lesser extent affected by the turmoil, even though the degree of contagion and its gestation period vary from country to country.

As an international response to the crisis, a number of rescue packages with an attached major reform agenda and with substantial funding from the International Monetary Fund (IMF), the World Bank (WB), the Asian Development Bank (ADB) and other international institutions have been arduously negotiated and then produced for the countries in trouble. A number of financial and banking reforms has also been suggested by international authorities and governments for the countries that are likely to be next in the list of a major economic crisis. It is our view and the view of many experts and authorities in the world economies that these remedies and reforms have not been so effective when adopted and implemented in restoring the path of growth in the countries in turmoil, or even in halting the crisis' relentless march itself either in Asia or in other parts of the world. What are then the prospects of the countries in crisis and other countries in the neighbourhood or in the distance that have been affected by the crisis both in the short- and long-term time-frame?

This chapter gives an overview of the principal causes of the crisis, their rescue or reform packages and the outcomes over the past fifteen months or so in the major Asian economies in turmoil. The prospects for all these countries as well as their trading countries will be critically analysed and reported with available data and relevant knowledge gathered since the crisis emerged. The analysis will provide substantive information for use by government planners, policy-makers, business executives, institutional experts and all individuals interested in growth, development, international trade and investment in a national and global context.

2.　Alternative diagnoses and management of the crisis

At the beginning, the Asia crisis was likened to that happening in Mexico in the early and mid-1990s. The causes of both crises were diagnosed as similar by the IMF (Camdessus, President of the IMF, on the Australian Broadcasting Commission [ABC] television, early in 1998) and many economic analysts worldwide: a sudden and large capital outflow from the countries involved. While it is easy to argue that capital outflows may have directly caused the devaluation of the local currency or the insolvency of many corporations or banking institutions operating in some Asian countries in trouble, these outflows could be the final conduit of other deeper causes and they reflect more appropriately these fundamental problems that have been underlying the movement of short-term capital by international fund or bank managers from one country to another. Some of these fundamental problems, to name a few, are: the differential in the prevailing interest rates in different countries, the free movement of especially short-term capital across the countries, government fiscal and monetary policy, a lack of good governance, currency speculation, and a misallocation of investment funds to wrong projects or sectors. There is a strong case to argue that two other fundamentals important in this case, which have not been adequately raised or discussed, are: the immaturity of the financial market in the economies in crisis and the inadequacies, failures or unfettered excesses of economic and financial globalization (see, however, a brief mention of the latter in Wiseman [1998]).

From a new perspective of the IMF, the Asian countries in crisis (Indonesia, Thailand, Korea, the Philippines and Malaysia) are the victims of their own successes (Aghevli, 1998) and their problems are distinct from those of the Latin American economies in the mid-1990s. Thus, while the Latin American economies during this period suffered large government deficits, huge public debts, excessive monetary expansion and major structural problems, the East Asian countries in 1997 enjoyed big government surpluses and had no problem with public debts, money expansion or structural woes.

The fundamental causes of the Asia crisis again according to the IMF have been listed as: large foreign direct investment (FDI) diverted from a weak-growth Europe to a high-growth Asia, a weak banking system, a lack of good governance and transparency, a fixed exchange-rate regime, the gain of the US dollar against the Japanese yen, China's devaluation, North America Free Trade Area (NAFTA) export growth, and substantial capital inflows causing large current account deficits, large external debts and sharp fund withdrawals.

The IMF cures for these woes which are contained in its rescue packages include: the IMF be the liquidity provider, the interest rate should be kept high and financial reforms be carried out (including the closure of bad banks and corporate restructuring). Strangely, the IMF claims that these cures often fit in well with the Asian governments' agenda for changes and were supported by them for implementation (Aghevli, 1998).

International critics of the IMF's rescue programmes are predictably numerous and they range from the WB economists to national central bank governors, economic research institute analysts and other individual financial and economic experts.

These critics claim that the IMF's policy of shutting down banks has caused panic, as in the 1930s Great Depression, and it has not arrested the turmoil. The IMF should have lent money to the Asian economies in trouble to calm the public and the investors. The problem in East Asia is akin to a bank run, and no country in the world is strong enough to withstand such a run. The IMF claimed, as a basis for its rescue policy, that the governments in East Asia had lived beyond their means, but on evidence, it was the private sector that was deeply in debt and to blame. In this case, the orthodox medicine of government budget cuts and credit restrictions were inappropriate.

These critics (for example, Sachs, 1997 and Radelet and Sachs, 1998) diagnosed the East Asian economies as having not only big government surpluses, but high savings, low taxes, a flexible labour market, and large foreign reserves. The real causes of the Asia crisis were China's competition and slow export growth in the years immediately before the crash. It was the financial sector and not the Asian governments' folly that generated the meltdown as we know it.

3.   The effectiveness of the crisis management

At the time of writing, it appears that the various rescue packages imposed by the IMF on the Asian countries in crisis have not had the effect they were intended to have. On the contrary, these packages have caused considerable hardships for the grass-roots people of the countries concerned, have toppled the government in two major economies in the region, and have not stopped the contagion from spreading beyond East Asia, to Russia and Brazil. This poignant observation applies to all of the countries in crisis and these include the economies that seem to have arrested the meltdown, namely, Thailand and Korea. In the more specific case of Malaysia, by the second quarter of 1998, the economy, after adopting the IMF packages, had shrunk by 6.8 per cent and the forecast was negative for the rest of the year, the ringgit (the Malaysian dollar) had lost 40 per cent of its original value against the US dollar, and the country had lost A\$ 60 billion in terms of its GDP due to devaluation.

The IMF blamed the ineffectiveness of its packages on the problems it had encountered since the 7 were put in place: a lack of early information and transparency to monitor the economy in East Asia, the important role of the financial institutions in the global economy, fixed exchange rate inflexibility, capital market liberalization, and a lack of fund for the IMF (Aghevli, 1998).

The IMF exponents (such as Sachs, 1997) point out that the failure of the IMF packages are due solely to its wrong diagnosis of the Asia crisis and, subsequently, the wrong prescriptions. The cures for the crisis according to these exponents are opposite to what the IMF has advocated and acted upon, and they would have had better outcomes in dealing with the crisis had they been adopted: let the exchange rates float, follow a slight monetary expansion policy and increase the competitiveness. A local currency devaluation will bring about cheaper exports, more FDI into the country, and lower interest rates as the funds become abundant (Sachs, 1997).

It is worth emphasizing here that the diagnoses and the cures for the Asia crisis adopted or proposed above by the IMF and its exponents are basically informal and non-databased. They are formulated on the basis of short-term data correlation analysis (e.g., corporate bankruptcies are related to the inability to pay, currency devaluation is related to a decline in international reserves) and unsubstantiated or hypothesized causal directionality (e.g., speculative funds cause the Asia crisis, bad governance generates capital outflows) between the economic and financial aggregates of interest. While this kind of approach to an economic or financial crisis can be useful for arm-chair discussions and *ad hoc* policy formulation and implementation, it can never ensure a definite outcome since it may not be able to identify and verify the real cause (or causes) of the turmoil.

Unfortunately for our proper and deep understanding of the Asia turmoil or even the Mexico crisis (the latter and its cures have been used by the IMF and other analysts to justify their prescriptions for East Asia problems), serious empirical studies of the fundamental causes of the 1997 Asia meltdown or even of the Mexico crisis of 1994/95 have not been rigorously carried out and reported. (See the Asia Crisis, *The Internet*, 1998. See also the exception to this in Van Hoa and Harvie, 1999.) When the causes are not properly diagnosed, the cures would be necessarily inappropriate, and the effectiveness of these cures would be a fluke if it actually were to occur.

From our recent empirical findings for the major Asian economies in crisis (Van Hoa and Harvie, 1999), it appears that many aspects of the IMF rescue packages or of other prescriptions proposed by analysts and commentators have no supporting statistical and historical evidence. For example, our findings indicate that the government sector in these countries generally had no significant role in affecting growth or inflation. A rescue policy that relies heavily on the premise that this sector was to blame for the turmoil in the economies in question is therefore misplaced and, as a result, ineffective in redressing the problem.

4. The worldwide prospects after the Asia Crisis

The analysis of the crisis and its remedial management discussed above from both the informal and data-based, or historical, perspectives appears to indicate that the prospects for Asia and the rest of the world are rather pessimistic in the next few years. This view can be attenuated somewhat, however, if an extensive study is undertaken to pinpoint the real causes of the Asia crisis on a country-by-country basis, to formulate suitable rescue policy and to have better and more appropriate prescriptions for its ills. A concerted effort by the international community as a whole is also required to spur growth (by for example introducing an interest-rate cut), development and other economic activities in a global context.

From an informal or analytical perspective, the IMF rescue packages have not been able to arrest the turmoil in many East Asian countries or to stop it from spreading to other countries in Asia and beyond. In fact, only a few months ago, Malaysia, a major economy in the Association of the South East Asian Nations (ASEAN), decided to cut its trading and financial ties from the rest of the world as it was unhappy with the negligible outcomes as a result of adopting the IMF rescue packages and it was also concerned with the influence the international capital market was exerting on Malaysia in particular. It achieved this by introducing strict credit regulations and currency controls or, in fact, by abandoning an open-door trade policy. The policy has been criticized by free-market analysts and governments as being short-sighted and isolationist with damaging prospects for development, trade and investment in Malaysia and for international economic relations. While the policy may succeed in restarting the Malaysian economy in the short run, but in the long run a shortage of FDI and with it a reduction in advanced-technology transfers and human-resource development enhancement may do more harm to the economy than is anticipated by the Malaysian authorities. Part of this policy has also been blamed for creating events leading to the social and political unrest in the peninsular in the past few months, with wide regional and international repercussions.

From a data-based and historical approach, the findings appear to support the views (1) that international trade, FDI and other international business activities have generated high growth in the Asian region and (2) that the public sector has played a nearly insignificant role in it. On the basis of these findings, it is the private sector with its national and especially international economic activities and not the government with its interventionist role that has been the dominating force in promoting the remarkable economic achievements in the region in the past three decades or so. It is therefore logical in this context to venture a hypothesis that the prospects for Malaysia when it adopts an isolationist policy are not rosy and its people are the real losers in the years to come. In addition, a policy which squarely puts the blame for the crisis on only the government seems misplaced. A subsequent remedy of 'fixing the government's management first and all other economic woes will disappear' has no substantive support and its expected outcomes of being able to solve the crisis have to be merely wishful thinking.

It is interesting to note in the case of Thailand that after generating the crisis which has world-wide contagion implications, the country seems to have restored the economy to the path of positive growth and development in recent months. The value of the baht (Thailand's currency) has reclaimed most of its loss after the July 1997 crisis and the political situation has improved. This kind of recovery has been achieved, according to many local and international analysts, by the effort of the government to restructure the banking and financial system, by the action of the business sector to downsize investment and, importantly, by the local community to develop what has been known as the self-help (domestically oriented) programme with support from the king and the country's leading economists. A combination of some belt-tightening policy, a stricter control and better supervision of the banks and financial institutions, a reallocation of investment funds to economically viable projects, and a national programme of more domestic production and consumption, with less dependence on international trade activities, seems to have generated optimism and more positive prospects for Thailand.

5.   Worldwide plan for economic growth and financial reform

In spite of the positive achievements by some Asian countries after the crisis, the prospects for other Asian countries and the rest of the world as analytically and empirically evaluated have not been good and immediate action is needed to improve them. Government leaders, business executives, financial analysts and academics have often acknowledged this assessment either as a group or as individual commentators. At a recent (12–14 October 1998) East Asia Summit conference organized by the World Economic Forum in Singapore, the participants (about 1000 business leaders and government officials world wide) discussed the burning issues of trade and growth and proposed an action plan for global growth (the target) and reform of the world financial system (a chief determinant of the crisis). This plan recognizes the importance of international trade, the interrelationship of international economic activities and the role played by major advanced economies in the world economy. The plan (*World Economic Forum*, Internet, October 1998) includes the following recommendations:

- The US, Canada and Europe should adopt significant cuts in interest rates, and Japan should further expand its money supply, in order to bolster their own economies and the world economy against the rising threat of global recession.
- The Summit participants stress that Japan, as Asia's major high-income economy (supported chiefly by strong domestic activities and large positive balance-of-payments transactions), with a GNP twice as large as all of the rest of Asia combined, has a special responsibility to help the region emerge from its current deep recession. This can be achieved through a recapitalization of its financial sector, using public funds as needed to ensure a speedy recovery of the banking sector and adopting a dynamic and growth-promoting fiscal policy with an emphasis on expanding domestic consumption.

- Europe, Canada and the US should be prepared to adopt more expansionary fiscal policies, especially tax cuts, in the event that the growth outlook in the respective economies deteriorates still further.
- The advanced or developed economies should immediately expand the provision of official loans and credit guarantees to the emerging markets in crisis, especially to cover basic necessities in foodstuffs, energy, and medical and pharmaceutical supplies.
- The Miyazawa Plan should be supported to provide $US 30 billion in Japanese assistance to the crisis countries of East Asia and perhaps more if the contractionary forces in East Asia continue to gain momentum.
- Europe, the US, Canada and Japan should reconfirm their commitment to open trade in goods and services and to use safeguards (e.g., anti-dumping measures as the crisis is leading to significant shifts in trade flows) so as to support the emerging market economies in generating current account surpluses to restore their financial balance.
- Governments in the crisis countries of East Asia should commit to maintaining open markets for goods and services, recognizing that they would be the biggest losers in the worldwide lurch towards protectionism or isolationism.
- The crisis economies in Asia should, on their part, accelerate the recapitalization of their financial and banking sectors through an infusion of public funds and the involvement of new investors, domestic and foreign, in the ownership and control of domestic banks and financial firms.
- Korea and Thailand, which currently enjoy low inflation and high current account surpluses, should adopt expansionary monetary and fiscal policies to promote a return to positive growth.
- The crisis countries in Asia should facilitate the rapid restructuring of corporate debts in a pragmatic manner that recognizes the legitimate interests of both creditors and debtors.
- Governments in the crisis countries of East Asia should commit themselves to further openness to FDI, more transparency and strengthened institutional infrastructure, including in sectors that were previously restricted to foreign ownership, such as banking, and infrastructure where such limits still exist. These

sectors have played a critical part through the infusion of new capital and technology for stability and long-term growth.

- Countries should undertake to establish a new regulatory regime for the monitoring, disclosure and regulation of highly leveraged short-term financial flows as well as off-balance-sheet commitments and derivative transactions.
- The need for a comprehensive reconsideration by the IMF membership of the IMF and WB of the mandate, structures, functions and resources of these institutions, with the view of rendering them more accountable and transparent in their own operations and objectives and supportive of an open world economy.
- A global growth summit is needed but the emerging market economies should be equally represented along with the advanced economies at such a summit. This summit should be the starting-point for the elaboration of a new, world financial architecture.

6.   Conclusions

Due partly to the Asia crisis and its contagion, the world economy now is undergoing a process of instability and uncertainty and the prospects for a positive growth in the next few years are dim. Measures to reduce the impact of the crisis at the national level and to arrest the spreading of the turmoil at the international level are important but these measures may have not been properly prescribed because the real causes of the meltdown have not been accurately identified in a rigorous manner for even a specific country. While the financial market has been blamed for contributing to the emergence of the crisis, it may be the case that the operation and management of the financial system, a lack of sufficient prudential control and supervision, and cultural make-up have been the real causal factors.

These issues are important but a serious study of all of them for each of the world economies in crisis, or on the verge of having an economic crisis, would be monumental and difficult. This is particularly true when the information and data relevant to these issues are scarce or even unavailable to the public and even to the IMF itself in the case of Thailand as it has been claimed late in 1997 by Stanley Fischer, a deputy director of the IMF. Until such problems have been resolved, our diagnosis of the Asia crisis, its contagion and the prescriptions for it have to be regarded as simply proxies and second best.

In this scenario of the crisis and its proxy causes and cures, the prospects for renewed growth and international trade and investment are only rough guesses and of a qualitative nature. The prospects for Asia and the world economy in this case are nevertheless less than promising. The world economies led by the G7 recognize this, but even a concerted effort in the third quarter of 1998 as spearheaded by Alan Greenspan of the US Federal Reserve Board – the world's number one banker – and the US government to mount a cut in the prime interest rate and spur world growth has not brought about any consensus among the world economies. It appears that until such a concerted effort is agreed upon and quickly implemented to combat the crisis and its contagion, the prospects for the world economy remains bleak in the years to come.

References

Aghevli, B. B. (1998), *Asian Crisis: Causes and Remedies*, IMF, paper delivered at the Research Institute for Asia and the Pacific, University of Sydney, 1 July 1998.

Radelet, S. and Sachs, J. D. (1998), 'The East Asia Financial Crisis: Diagnosis, Remedies, Prospects', Harvard Institute for International Development, *Internet*, July 1998.

Sachs, J.D. (1997), *The Wrong Medicine for Asia*, *Internet*, September 1998.

Van Hoa, T. and Harvie, C. (1999), *Causes and Impact of the Asian Financial Crisis*, London: Macmillan.

Wiseman, J. (1998), *Global Nation? Australia and the Politics of Globalization*, Cambridge: Cambridge University Press.

World Economic Forum, *Internet*, October 1998.

3

The Financial and Economic Crisis in Thailand: Policy Responses, Social Impact and Counter Measures

Kitti Limskul

1. Introduction

The regional economic expansion and interdependence which were mainly driven by GDP growth of ASEAN (Association of South East Asian Nations) countries, the NIEs (newly industrialized economies) and China have come to interruption. The currency crisis or, in other words, a balance-of-payment crisis started in Thailand and spilled over into other neighbouring countries. The contagion effect in each national economy has proved that the regional economies are more highly interwoven than we have anticipated. The countries which are in the core of crisis, such as Thailand, Indonesia and Korea, are continuing to face difficulties alike. That is to say, they are facing capital flight, liquidity crunch, bankruptcies and lay-offs. The contagion effects may be worse than we have first predicted, especially the impact on the social sector which can be observed from massive lay-offs and unemployment in each particularly affected country.

The object of this chapter is to discuss briefly the causes of the economic and financial crisis which in the case of Thailand can be generalized to explain the regional crisis as well. More importantly, we would like to explore the impact on the social sector, especially the lay-offs and unemployment which are currently deteriorating in Thailand. We would like to survey the immediate and concrete responses from the government agencies and see whether these measures have properly resolved the effects of this social impact.

2.   The current situation and causes of crisis

2.1   The on-going financial and economic crisis, July 1997–May 1998

The Thai currency (baht) was floated in July 1997. It has brought about economic adjustments in Thailand under a *de facto* devaluation. The currency crisis was virtually the balance-of-payment crisis. Consequently, Thailand had to ask for a Stand-by Credit Arrangement, a rescue package of $US 4000 m from the International Monetary Fund (IMF) and from other countries under the IMF package. The total bail-out fund was $US 17.2 b.

As a matter of fact, Thailand had enjoyed a rather long period of high growth from 1986–1995. There was a short-term business cycle fluctuation in 1990–92 reaching its peak in 1995 and contracting thereafter. The cyclical downswings had not yet reached their limit in 1997 and it was predicted that the cycle would reach its cyclical trough at the end of 1998, if the exchange and interest rates would properly managed such that the liquidity crunch would be solved. The real sector would also be revived.

It is clear that the Ministry of Finance and the Bank of Thailand (BOT) have chosen to stabilize the exchange rate by intervening to keep high interest rates. Liquidity crunch discouraged the effort of the Ministry of Commerce in stimulating production and exports in the real sector. The monetary authorities were afraid that the inflation rate rise from 10 to 15 per cent per annum predicted by the IMF would finally cause the 'negative real rate effect' (inflation is higher than the prevailing interest rate). If that is the case, consumers may expect that prices will be spirally increased. It thereby reduces the saving ability of private households.

In fact, the *de facto* devaluation had forced the baht to depreciate by 50 per cent at the end of October 1997. The spot exchange rate was 41 baht per one US dollar as compared to 26.5 baht during the middle of July 1977. The Thai currency was not stable at the time and depreciated further due to massive capital outflows. As firms and banks started to repay their foreign borrowings, exporters and

investors were reluctant to hold baht for fear of further depreciation. The Ministry of Finance and the BOT had responded to this
by restoring a high interest-rate policy as the main core of their stabilization policy following the IMF's guidelines in the *Letter of Intent*.
During November–December 1997 and January–February 1998,
Thailand had faced severe volatile exchange rates with massive
capital outflows. However, during March and April 1998, the Thai
currency proved to be solidly stable at the rate of 39–41 baht per US
dollar. This was partially a result of a high interest-rate policy where
the minimum loan rate was approximately 16–17 per cent per
annum. In fact, the interest rate was kept high owing to two main
reasons. First, stabilizing the exchange rate was acceptable in so far
as the inflation rate was actually high and avoided a negative real
interest rate. The second reason, which was a crucial factor to induce
high interest rates, was simply that the Thai money market was distorted. The demand for funds by small state banks and the Financial
Institution Development Fund (FIDF) had caused short-term interest
rates to be higher than long-term interest rates. This 'inverted yield
curve effect' reflects a structural distortion in the money and
financial markets. The liquidity crunch caused bankruptcies and in
turn fed back to the banks' ability to manage their balance-sheet. The
non-performing loans were predicted to increase substantially.

The baht devaluation had turned the trade balance from deficit to
surplus. Exports had recovered as expected just after the devaluation, even when measured in real or dollar terms. This 'J-Curve
Effect' signified that exports increased, while imports decreased as a
result of devaluation until the end of 1997. However, during the
first quarter of 1998 imports decreased at a faster rate than exports
increased in absolute terms. The balance of trade and current
account have shown an unsatisfactory improvement despite
exports' tendency to decline, in dollar terms. This was because
financial credit is not generally accessible to small and medium
firms. Imports which were inputs for the production of exports were
not properly procured. Exports tended to increase with a decreasing
rate, and finally declined. Unless high interest rates and tight credit
extension are relaxed, exports may not expand as primarily
expected. Thus, the depth of the business-cycle trough of the Thai
economy may be prolonged, and the economy may not bottom out
as soon as had been expected.

The lack of trustworthiness of the financial system for local and international creditors has caused a fast deterioration of assets quality and a systemic risk of insolvency of the financial institutions and vice versa. In fact, the insolvency of financial institutions was caused by their highly leveraged structure: a high debt/equity ratio resulting in the high costs of financial distress. The credit extension by financial institutions was largely financed by a significant amount of foreign borrowing through the channel of BIBF (Bangkok International Banking Facilities) by the private sector at $US 90 000 million as of July 1997. Major borrowing was destined for the financing of capital investment in the private sector, thereby making excess production capacity in the various industrial sectors in excess of 10 per cent. Part of the total outstanding foreign private debt was to finance the real estate development in recent years, as well as extravagant consumption, of the new rich in Thailand.

The moral hazard and the capital flight have caused the fluctuations of the exchange rate and excess liquidity needed by the real sector. The pressure from the creditors has caused financial distress and moral hazard as well as capital flight. This vicious cycle was partly solved by the authorities in March 1998 when Thailand complied with the IMF's demand as written in the third letter of intent. This is to set the path for recapitalization of the banking system. By the end of May 1998, another five decrees based on the Cabinet's decision on financial reforms were announced. Under these decrees, the Ministry of Finance will be allowed to restructure the short-term and long-term interest rate distortions or the 'inverted yield curve effect'. It will try to turn the FIDF into a Deposit Insurance Institution by capitalizing on the costs of interest and the principal of debts of the FIDF through fiscalized bonds under the agreement in the letter of intent.

The insolvency crisis, distressing 56 finance companies that were temporarily suspended, has been solved transparently with their on-going asset auction. In addition, the FIDF's seizure of collaterals from the finance companies was revoked since the creditors demanded that it violates the 'rule of negative pledge'. The former government has initiated to promulgate five royal decrees as follows: (1) Financial Institution Restructure Act B.E. 2540; (2) Asset Management of Financial Institution Act B.E. 2540; (3) Amendment of Bank of Thailand Act, B.E. 2485 (second issue), B.E. 2540; (4) Amendment of Commercial Bank Act B.E. 2508 (third issue), B.E. 2540; Amendment of Finance and Security Company and Credit Frontier Act, B.E. 2522 (fourth issue) B.E. 2540; and (5) Tax Code Act (k 17) B.E. 2540. These decrees were for the sake of restructuring the financial system. First, the government has set up a Financial Restructure Agency (FRA) to solve the 58 finance companies insolvency problem. Second, the government will set up a corporation called Radhanasin Bank and Asset Management Corporation (AMC) to monitor and liquidate good and bad assets and liabilities respectively of the 56 suspended finance companies. Third, under the amended Bank of Thailand Act, the FIDF and other creditors will have equal claims on seized assets. In addition, it also gives an authority to supervise the remaining 33 finance companies which were not suspended as well as 15 commercial banks. As a matter of fact, during the economic downswings, these institutions' non-performing loans (NPL) may also be high or, in other words, their asset quality may deteriorate too. Currently, two large banks have partly raised capital and other banks are trying re-capitalization as well. Other banks were scheduled to increase their capital by the end of 1998. As of May 1998, two out of 58 finance companies were allowed to continue their operation, while four small banks were consolidated to be government banks after being forced to write down their former shares. These four small government banks are trying to pay back loans to the FIDF. This is done by attracting deposits with overly high interest rates. Larger banks have responded by increasing deposit rates. This fierce competition has adversely affected and caused distortions in the money and financial markets.

In May 1998, the government remitted a better signal of crisis management. The government tried to solve the currency crisis (unstable exchange rates) simultaneously with the balance-of-payment crisis (current account deficit, external debt service and domestic liquidity problems) and the financial institution crisis (insolvency problem of financial institutions). The government is pursuing with financial reforms; although avoiding an intervention in the negotiation between private foreign creditors and private domestic debtors to roll over debts, still the government has tried to put forward dialogues between creditors and debtors domestically. They also tried to soften the classification of loans and reserves by private banks, although it is clear that the government aimed at facilitating the talk rather than bearing the debt burden of the private sector. At the end of March 1998 some large amount of private debts were rolled-over. A series of reforms were promised by the government, such as privatization, restructuring of the BOT, amending the alien laws to allow foreigners to run a certain kind of economic activities with an additional occupation permit, introducing the bankruptcies and foreclosure laws, etc.

The effort being pursued by the government has brought about confidence in general, both domestically and abroad. The IMF has agreed to provide Thailand with the third portion of loans to help restore the foreign currency reserves of the country. The exchange rate between the baht and the US dollar was stabilized around the 40 baht per dollar during the first quarter of 1998, but at the cost of tight liquidity and bankruptcies of small and medium companies. Export and import financial credit had been thought to revive but its recovery did not materialize as merchandise exports in dollar terms have been declining. Despite the inflow of loans through a co-financing of private international banks, mostly European and Japanese, under the arrangement of the ADB and the import credit from the ExIm Bank (for export and imports) of the US after the visit of Prime Minister Chuan in March 1998, it seems that the liquidity drain was the most destabilizing factor that was causing the severe economic crisis, shut-downs, lay-offs and other social impact during this currency crisis.

Thus, by the end of April 1998, it was realized that the policy, resolutions and measures were in general in the right direction but they were not optimal. Interest rates were too high as the money market had been distorted by the FIDF's intervention. In fact, inflation was proclaimed to be virtually manageable, and lower than expected. In this case, the 'negative real rate effect' should not be invoked as announced. There was mounting pressure from the private non-financial sector to lower the general interest-rate level. The Ministry of Finance therefore launched 15 measures to help solve the liquidity problem and fix the distortion in the money market. For fear of weakening the growth trend of exports (in dollar terms), the government may try to relax the high interest-rate and tight liquidity policies but not before asking the consent of the IMF. During May 1998, the IMF mission came to evaluate the achievement of its rescue package for the fourth payment. Liquidity and bankruptcies *vis-à-vis* high interest and exchange rates stabilization policy were in the top agenda.

2.2 The root of the currency crisis in the Asian region

The root of crisis in the region can be singled out from that occurring in Thailand and the common features that the regional economy have, after allowing for the difference due to the different stages of development. The crisis started in Thailand due to the monetary authorities' own macroeconomic mismanagement as a result of using contradicting policy instruments. The intra-regional and inter-regional factors were also the determinants of the turmoil in the region. The following chronology will be noted so that the timeframe of the discussion will be clearly demarcated.

2.2.1 The root of the currency crisis in Thailand

(a) Rapid economic growth has caused the widening of the investment-saving gap. Identically, this is a current account deterioration gap. Thailand's rapid economic development after 1985 has caused a huge influx of foreign direct investment. This has occurred as a result of the realignment of the exchange rate between the Japanese yen and US dollar and other key currencies after the Plaza Accord meeting in 1985. The improved economic condition has caused an increase of private consumption. As a result, this has caused the lessening of saving potential of the households. The household saving has declined significantly to be just 6–8 per cent of GDP in recent years. The rapid economic growth needed a stimulus from rising investment, thus the investment-saving gap has been widened. Identically, this is a current account gap. It has been deteriorated to the level of 8–9 per cent of GDP in 1996.

(b) Policy failures, misled economic signal, and incongruent economic philosophy with the globalization mega-trend. Thailand's national economic policy has set a rather high average growth target of 8 per cent per annual. With this growth rate during 1996–2000, Thailand would need a huge source of investment finance which it could not finance by its own savings. Clearly, the rapid growth we aimed for will deteriorate from the current account position. The foreign saving has been our primary source of investment finance. Thus, before the crisis break-out in July 1997, Thailand had had external debts of $US 90 billion, 70 billion dollars of which were in the private sector. Here, 40 per cent was short-term in nature and had to be rolled over every 3 months. The corporate planners seemed to

enjoy 8 consecutive years of cash surplus in its fiscal side. Thus, the private sector was allowed to borrow funds at cheap costs from off-shore sources through the facility called BIBF (Bangkok International Banking Facilities) and then to re-lend them to finance local projects using a high interest differential. The planned growth target implied a rising income and consumption domestically. This has made the domestic market for non-tradeable goods expand significantly as the reversed term-of-trade between tradeable and non-tradeable price ratios has become favourable to the non-tradeable goods and services, such as the services derived from having mobile telephones, private cars and owning properties. Easy funding has made speculation of shares in the stock market, land and other durable goods a booming activity.

Time frame	Economic epoch and trend
1975–1985	It was a period of high economic growth after the first oil crisis and commodities boom. The Thai economy was severely affected by the *second oil crisis*. The business cyclical downswing was alternating with recovery. In 1984/85, the economy entered the most depressed situation. The Thai baht was devalued twice and later pegged to a basket of currencies with 70 per cent of it in dollars.
1986–1990	After the *Plaza Accord*, the realignment of key currency yen has been forced to appreciate. Influx of foreign direct investment to Southeast Asia. Private investment growth of 20–30 per cent and export growth of 29 per cent were observed in Thailand. Domestic market grew considerably as a result of income expansion in export oriented activities.

Time frame	Economic epoch and trend
1990–1992	*Financial liberalization phase I*, by relaxing the controls on interest rates, allowing more flexibility in the capital account and the emergence of capital market. As a result, capital flowed in to finance domestic demand oriented activities. Firms now could seek capital raising by leveraging in money and capital market. As conspicuous consumption rose, household saving fell, making the current account deficit deteriorate.
1993–1994	*Financial liberalization phase II*, under the international banking facility *BIBF*, capital inflows were intended to be manipulated through Bangkok called 'out-out' facilities, however, in most cases it was an 'out-in' flow, with very scant 'in-out' activities. The excess supply of capital inflow in both FDI and portfolio investment created a situation of excess liquidity supply, with booming real estate and stock market. Most firms which could access international money and capital market through BIBF fell into high leveraged corporations. The monetary policy was ineffective, a high interest-rate policy could not squeeze liquidity as capital inflow was indefinitely increasing. High domestic interest rates caused interest rate arbitrage and large capital inflows, while a pegged exchange system which was intended to stabilize export earnings was a contradiction in nature. It reduced the exchange rate

Time frame	Economic epoch and trend
1995–1996 (1st half)	risk of capital inflows and outflows to a virtually 'risk free' one. High interest rates did not hamper domestic demand expansion as liquidity could be raised from foreign funds. Terms-of-trade shifted in favour of non-tradeable goods such as real estate and consumer durable goods through hire purchase systems. Thus, household saving was clearly deteriorating, and overburdening the current account deficit. Most large firms with capital investment (mostly in the stock market) faced an over-capacity situation as they turned to the domestic market, however, as relative prices were infavour of domestic demand as a result of overvalued exchange rates, imports still increased, while exports had shown a weakening trend. Corporate operating performance had been deteriorating. Unfortunately, massive capital inflows had prolonged the bad businesses from a crash. Bad performance companies had to seek refinancing. Investors started to notice the inability to pay back loans as exports did not show a strong increasing sign, and later collapsed to non-positive growth.
1996 (2nd half)–1997	The non-performing loans of the financial sector were increasing fast, portfolio quality had been deteriorating, and the currency was under attack. The authority tried to defend the currency with counter-intervention into the markets. Financial crisis and credit

Time frame	Economic epoch and trend
	crunch were overwhelming, systemic risk and contagion effects spread throughout the economy. The authority resorted to swap instrument to counter the currency attack, while opening up baht-accumulating channels to attackers, thereby called in mounting attacks with definitely huge mobilized international funds. They had finally defeated Thailand in its currency war absolutely by May 1997. In July 1997, the Thai currency had floated or *de facto* devalued. Thailand had to ask for a bailout package from the IMF soon after the float.

Since the public sector believed that the private provision of public goods, such as telephone services, electricity, tollways and expressways, was a good thing, it stopped the public burden in the development of infrastructure in the urban area. The capital accumulation of the public and private sectors has been shifted from the previous trend laid down by the National Plan. The easy money has caused firms to be overleveraged and indebted deeply. The commercial banks and non-bank financial sector have fallen into the pitfall of the bubble and they were the intermediaries in financial deals. The high costs of funds to non-bank finance companies had difficulties as these companies' non-performing loans increased to the threshold.

Under the BIBF, the financial market was liberalized, and only the incoming fund was welcomed; the outgoing fund was not blessed. The easy money came to an end when the external sector, which is export-earning, had shown sign of deterioration in 1995/96, in addition to the signal of the large current account deficit. The misleading economic policy could be seen from the two prongs. These were a high interest-rate policy and a fixed exchange-rate policy while the financial market was partially liberalized to allow financial capital influx without a proper supervision by the authority as mentioned earlier. This clearly meant that funds could be shifted in and out of the country without an exchange risk, despite a large margin of interest gap between on-shore and off-shore capital. Despite frequent outcries from exporters and academics that the Thai baht was overvalued, the response was minimal from the BOT who oversaw the exchange-rate policy. The BOT mistakenly made a policy mix, that is to have a stabilized exchange rate (to drive exports) on the one hand, and luring off-shore funds from abroad to finance investment locally by having set high domestic interest rates on the other hand. These were contradicting targets and policy choices. Thus, the exchange rate was a signal that Thailand will never devalue the baht and/or float its currency. The Ministry of Finance was also not careful enough to implement a strict counter-cyclical policy, rather it only satisfied itself with the automatic stabilization of tax revenue increases as a result of overbooming economic activities.

The incongruent economic policy with the rapid pace of globalization in the financial world could be seen from the philosophy that financial institutions could never be bankrupted. This was the belief that was insistently practised by our monetary authority. This was a correct policy if and only if the world financial market was not interdependent as it is today. The global financial market can be linked together through computer networks. The trading activities are 24 hours per day. Besides, the US dollar which is only a paper money is being valued as a store of value as well as an exchange medium. The trading of the US dollar as a commodity in itself is much larger than that as a medium nomination for trading goods. The foreseeable devaluation trend has called in the currency attackers. And they did really win the battle. The central bank had lost huge sums from total currency forwards and swaps totalling $US 23.4 billion. Before July 1997, when the baht was *de facto* devalued, Thailand had $US 33 billion in foreign currency reserves.

After the currency crisis, it was the turn of the financial institution crisis. The government had ordered a closedown of 56 finance companies and a re-capitalization of 4 medium-sized banks. The Financial Institution Development Fund had spent huge sums in financial loans to rescue the distressed non-bank financial companies as well as the commercial banks. The incongruent economic philosophy 'banks can never be bankrupted' went against the tide of mega-trends, that is, the global financial markets efficiently compete with one another, and this has put the financial system of Thailand on the verge of collapse.

2.2.2 The root of crisis from external sources

(a) The intra-regional factors. The sub-regional area, the ASEAN, the NIEs and China have had a common pattern of economic growth, that is, the export-led growth policy is the flagship of these countries in the region. The growth pattern imitated a lesson from the Japanese experience or miracle. Clearly, the growth pattern is not always a free trade but it is to push for export earnings. Thus, local industries may not be efficient and protected. Labour productivity may not be high enough to cover the high costs of capital. Rather, most of the countries have relied on cheap wages to stimulate its export of light industries. According to the Japanese pattern of growth, the so-called ' Flying Geese hypothesis', one country after another will repeat (or fly after) the same pattern of the forerunners (ahead of the group) according to the product cycle. Thailand has passed the light industrialization stage and started to substitute capital for labour in its various industries. Newcomers are Vietnam and China who are competing in textiles, garments and shoes. In 1994, China devalued its currency by 40 per cent. This has made Chinese goods very cheap as compared with goods from other parts of the ASEAN except Vietnam.

On the other side of the region, the Korean economy was entering a new phase of economic development to a higher capital-intensive and technological drive. Unfortunately, the Japanese yen, the head of the group, had depreciated against the US dollar in 1996 from its appreciation tendency as a result of huge trade and current account surpluses with the world and especially the US. Korean exports could not compete with those from ASEAN and China in lower technology and labour-intensive products. At the same time, it could not compete in higher technology products with Japan or the US. The reason was clear: Korea, Thailand, Indonesia and Malaysia had a very high debt/GDP ratio before the crisis as compared with the level in 1980. Thus, the influx of capital (either long- and short-term) have overvalued the exchange rates of these economies. In short, these countries have tried to jump over to a higher level of product cycle in economic development and, with insufficient domestic savings, they had to rely on foreign savings.

Currently, it is still a question whether most of the countries in the region have devalued their currencies to be at par with their implicit comparative advantages. Secondly, whether the exchange rate has been stable yet, or will there be another round of competing devaluation?

(b) The inter-regional factors.   The inter-regional factors can be seen from the fact that as the yen has depreciated against the US dollar, Japan has run a trade surplus with the US and the world. The accumulation of the surplus could not be recycled efficiently. This is because the banking and financial system in Japan is lagging behind the global financial market like the US or UK. Thus, one part of the financial assets was kept in the banking sector inside Japan while the other part was seeking opportunities abroad, that is, to invest in Treasury bond in the US market. While the US ran a trade deficit, Japan and some Asian countries, after gaining more dollars, would now finance the US trade deficit by investing in the bond, stock, and property market in the US. This clearly made the dollar appreciate. Then the next round of the vicious cycle began again. The depreciation of the yen lessened demand for imports from the ASEAN and NIEs while a strong dollar increased demand for imports but from countries where the currencies were weak. Surely, Thai exports were defeated by cheaper exports from China, Latin America and other ASEAN countries. Thus, in short, the intra-regional relation between the US and Japan has caused a disturbance to the regional economies.

(c) The global mega-trends.   The global mega-trends can be seen from the 24-hour trading financial market around the world. New rules or new orders are set by the US, whose financial market has acquired several structural changes since 1975. The world has to follow the name of the game which has been set. The IMF created after the meeting in Bretton Woods following World War II could not cope with new mega-trends, that is to say, the emergence of the investment banks and hedge funds who behave as if the world financial market is connected as one big market. The hedge funds do not have to comply with the global trading rules of financial transactions.

Since the rules do not exist so far, no solid world institution is responsible for the externalities caused by the roaming funds. In theory, the wealth (financial assets, foreign currency reserves) held by a small country in our region is seen by the currency attackers as a piece of virgin natural resources that can be accessed freely by exploiters. No solid property rights on financial assets and capital or foreign currency reserves are clearly defined. Most importantly, there is no world police (regulators) on the activity of these hedge funds on the global scale, across the national borders and across the regions. The question is: will these mega-trends be a new world order? Do we need another world institution to regulate this cross-border currency operation including currency attacks?

3. Social impact of the financial and economic crisis in Thailand

3.1 Size of social impact: lay-offs and estimated unemployment

The size of social impact is estimated as follows: 1) The NESDB (National Economic and Social Development Board) applied survey data from the National Statistical Office (NSO) to arrive at the unemployment figures for 1998. Given an economic decline of –3.5 per cent, the employment is 30.299 million persons as compared with 30.693 million persons in 1997. Employment in non-agriculture decreases to 16.016 million persons in 1998, from 16.516 million persons in 1997. The NESDB estimated that unemployment would be 977 thousand persons in 1998, as compared with 626 thousand persons in 1997, making the total unemployment ratio 2.95 per cent in 1998 as compared with 1.91 per cent in 1997.

The new entrants into the labour force who are facing no available jobs for them are concentrated in the lower secondary, 26.6 per cent, and the higher vocational, 20.7 per cent of the total new entrants.

A cooperative survey between the NESDB and the private sector's organizations has recorded a severed unemployment situation in almost every manufacturing sub-sector. The average unemployment ratio was 24.4 per cent at the end of the fourth quarter of 1997. The food, automobile and parts industries seem to have been severely hit by the crisis. Their unemployment ratios are 37.1 and 35.1 per cent respectively. The modern service sector, especially in security and finance, has an unemployment ratio of 45.9 per cent, while the construction sector has 50.5 per cent. In total, out of 1 442 449 persons, there are 421 529 persons or 29.2 per cent who are unemployed in the survey.

The Ministry of Interior surveyed unemployed persons in each village throughout the whole kingdom in January 1998. It reported that there are altogether 1 156 657 persons who were unemployed. Among these, 813 513 persons or 70.3 per cent are in agriculture sector. It further reported that in March 1998 there were 1 322 379 unemployed persons in the North, Northeast, Central, and South. Among these, 954 166 were in the agriculture sector, 175 134 in the manufacturing sector, and 193 079 persons were *U-turn* unemployed persons. In total, the current size of the crisis' social impact on employment is 1 899 519 persons in 1998.

The size of lay-offs and unemployment depends heavily on the speed of the business cyclical downswing. Based on the third letter of intent, the IMF has predicted that the Thai economy would slowdown with a GDP growth rate of –3.5 to –3.0 per cent per annum. With this growth rate, the level of employment is estimated by the NESDB as 0.977 million persons. However, as we have mentioned in the first section of this chapter – that the credit crunch exhibited by high interest rates and tight liquidity in the real sector was part of important austerity measures put forward by the IMF – there is a possibility that the economy will decline substantially faster and deeper than expected. This implies that the estimated figure of unemployment is correct as the NESDB has shown. The response of the true labour market is much more dynamic and volatile than the authority has perceived.

The NESDB has produced a number of estimates concerning the unemployment figures. The Brooker Group (13 March 1998, p. 7) has cited the NESDB's estimates under the same coordinated institutes. It came out that the unemployment rates were 3.54 and 5.6 per cent of total labour force in 1997 and 1998 respectively as compared with 1.54 per cent in 1996. These figures are quite different from those reported above. Even that the Brooker Group (13 March 1998, p. 6) commented that the rate remained relatively low when compared with that of other economies, such as the 5.9 per cent (4.7 per cent after seasonal adjustments) in February

Table 3.1 Labour force, employment and unemployment, 1998

Unit: 1000 persons

	1997^2	1998^e
1. Economic Growth Rates	–0.4	–3.5
2. Population	60 602	61 201
3. Labour Force	32 836	33 095
4. Employment[1]	30 693	30 299
Agriculture	14 133	14 283
Non-Agriculture	16 560	16 016
5. Unemployment	626	977
Open Unemployment, seeking for job	182	362
Do not seek for job, but ready to work	444	615
6. Under Employment (work less than 35 hours/		
week and would like to work more)	945	1 194
7. Waiting for Agricultural Season (average)	572	625
Off-Season	1 036	1 100
During Season (August)	106	150
8. Population not in Labour Force	13 810	14 145
9. Population Age under 13 years	13 956	13 961
10. New Entrant into Labour Force	545	577
11. Total Unemployment Rate	1.91	2.95
Registered unemployment (Open Unemployed)	0.55	1.09
Not looking for jobs but Ready to Work	1.35	1.86
12. Waiting for Agricultural Season	1.74	1.89
13. Participation Rates	70.39	70.06

Notes: 1 excluding under employment
      2 Average of Labour Force Survey 2 rounds
      e Estimated

Sources: Sub-Committee on the Projection of Labour Force, Employment, and Unemployment. The Committee comprises representatives from Ministry of Labour and Social Welfare, NESDB, NSO, Bank of Thailand TDRI, NEC, and Office of Agricultural Economics. (Released on 24 April 1998)

1998 in Korea reported by the National Statistical Office (1998) and cited by the International Labour Organization (ILO, April 1998, Table 2.4 p. 16). We tend to believe that the lay-offs will be increasing and unemployment will be larger than the estimated figures as the economy is spiralling downwards.

One component of unemployment is new entrants into the labour force. In 1998 there were 577 140 persons out of the education system as compared with 544 564 persons in 1997. It may be postulated that

Table 3.2   New entrants into labour force from the education system, 1997–98

Education level	1997	1998	1997 per cent	1998 per cent
Primary 6	98 016	59 931	18.00	10.38
Lower Secondary	181 054	153 884	33.25	26.66
Upper Secondary	31 463	75 143	5.78	13.02
Lower Vocational (Por-Wor-Chor)	49 791	62 128	9.14	10.77
Higher Vocational, (Por-Wor-Sor, Por-Wor-Tor)	98 006	119 505	18.00	20.71
University Under Graduate	86 234	106 549	15.83	18.46
All	544 564	577 140	100.0	100.0

Source: National Education Council, 1998

at the peak of the crisis nobody could find a job. Rather firms tended to reduce their work force to save costs if a wage cut could not actually help. The estimates by the Thai Farmers' Bank Research Center (reported in Chalamwong, 1998) were based on a negative GDP growth rate of –2.0 per cent and a 10 per cent inflation rate. It came up with a 1.919 million people unemployed across the sectors. Unemployment as a percentage of current employment in the construction sector is 13.45 per cent, in manufacturing 13.31 per cent, in services 9.6 per cent, in mining and quarrying 6.05 per cent, in transportation and communication 5.22 per cent, in agriculture 4.87 per cent and in utilities 3.48 per cent respectively.

The estimated unemployment figures are not very stable at all. They depend on the unstable growth rates sector by sector which are not truly observable. We first try to investigate the number of lay-offs. The government has ordered the Ministry of Interior to invent a system of labour market information, while the NESDB in cooperation with the associated institutions has carried out surveys on the lay-offs during the third and fourth quarters of 1997. The employment level in the surveyed firms was altogether 1.442 million persons, comprising 620 559 persons in the manufacturing, 500 000 persons in the construction sector and 321 890 persons in the modern services sector as of the third quarter of 1997. Those who were 'out of work' (and defined as 'lay-offs', forced retirees, and

Table 3.3 Officially and unofficially reported numbers of lay-offs during the third and fourth quarters of 1997

Sector	3rd Quarter		4th Quarter	Total	
	Employed persons	Out of work	Out of work	Out of work	per cent[4]
1. Manufacturing	620 559	119 620	31 837[3]	151 457	24.4
1.1 Chemical	40 000	12 000	*	12 000	30.0
1.2 Plastic	101 500	20 300	4 060	24 360	24.0
1.3 Rubber	39 400	–	7 880	7 880	20.0
1.4 Printing	57 357	20 000	*	20 000	34.9
1.5 Automobile and Parts	114 102	40 000	**	40 000	35.1
1.6 Electrics and Electronics	120 000	–	12 000	12 000	10.0
1.7 Shoes	54 000	2 828	***	2 828	5.2
1.8 Foods	94 200	24 492	10 456	34 948	37.1
2. Modern Services	321 890	9 483	8 089	17 572	5.5
2.1 Banking	122 979	615	*	615	0.5
2.2 Finance and Security[1]	24 594	5 304	6 000	11 304	45.9
2.3 Life and Non-Life Insurance	66 317	–	*	–	–
2.4 Export Business	N.A	–	N.A	–	–
2.5 Hotels	108 000	3 564	2 089	5 653	5.2
3. Construction[2]	500 000	87 500	165 000	252 500	50.5
All	1 442 449	216 603	204 926	421 529	29.2

Notes:
1. surveyed from 78 out of 91 securities and finance companies, as of October 1997
2. most of those who are laid-off are migrants from the agriculture sector after transplanting and harvesting, they are likely to return home and will be short of cash income earned
3. do not include those who will be retired from the spare parts and car assembly
4. percentage of laid-offs in two consecutive quarters over employed persons at end of third quarter
5. 'Out of work' include lay-off, forced retirees, and voluntary retired
'*' no additional recruitment '**' will decrease further, '***' increase 5 per cent.

Sources: Human Resource Department, NESDB with the cooperation with Federation of Industry, Thai Chamber of Commerce, Thai Construction Association, Personnel Club of Securities and Finance Company

Table 3.4 Estimated unemployment from surveyed data

Region	Unemployed in agriculture	Unemployed in non-agriculture	U-turn to place of origin	All
North	198 885	39 013	47 917	285 815
Northeast	706 167	98 036	120 871	925 074
Central	33 902	28 850	14 813	77 565
South	15 212	9 235	9 478	33 925
Sub-total	954 166	175 134	193 079	1 322 379
New Entrant into Labour Force				577 140
Estimated Total Unemployment				1 899 519
As per cent of total Labour Force (33.095 million)				5.73

Note: Part of laid-off workers are guest labours approximately 200 000–300 000 persons have retired and went back to their countries. Thus, the figures above are exclusive of foreign labours

Source: Regional data are surveyed by Ministry of Interior, New Entrants data are from NEC, see Table 3.2 above

voluntary retired during the third to the end of the fourth quarter) and combined together amounted to 421 529 persons or 29.2 per cent of total surveyed employment. The unemployment in the manufacturing was 24.4 per cent, while it was 50.5 per cent in the construction, but only 5.5 per cent in the modern services sector (although it was 49.5 per cent in the securities and finance sector). It should be noted that these unemployment figures will surely reflect in the tide of 'U-turn' to the rural area, if they are forced to do so, unemployment is not a luxurious leisure.

In Table 3.4 above we estimate the total unemployment level from the surveyed data of the Ministry of Interior. Regional unemployment reported by it was 1.32 million persons across the agriculture and non-agriculture sectors. This does not include 200–300 thousand foreign guest labourers who have gradually returned to their homelands. Assuming that the new entrants into the labour force from the education system are unfortunately jobless, the total estimated figures of unemployment were therefore 1.899 million persons. Given the number of the labour force, the unemployment ratio was approximately 5.73 per cent as of April 1998. If this figure is adjusted by the number of those who were waiting for the agricultural seasonal figure of 0.6 to 1.0 million persons, the net unemployment would be lowered to 0.8–1.2 million persons. From these figures are then subtracted those in open unemployment who were seeking jobs (0.36 million persons). Thus, the net unemployment is 0.5–0.8 or roughly 0.6 million persons on average. Note that the whole estimates must be changed as sectoral lay-offs were not accurately counted. So far, no institution in Thailand is able to demarcate the bottom of the business cycle, and the declining sectoral growth rates.

We have tried to estimate the change in the employment level during 1996–99 taking into account the economic crisis. The estimated figures stand for change in the demand for labour. The negative numbers indicate the *potential* lay-offs and unemployment. Given an economic growth of –3.1 per cent per annum, or close to the –3.0 to –3.5 per cent cited in the third Letter of Intent III, exports are predicted to grow 8 and 9.6 per cent at 1998 constant prices, private consumption expenditure decreases by –2.04 and –3.10 per cent per annum and gross fixed capital formation decreases by –1.9 and –8.8 per cent per annum during 1997 and 1998. The figures are at 1998 constant prices. Government expenditure decreases –21.37 per cent per annum in 1998. Therefore, final demand growth would be decreasing with a rate of –1.73 per cent in 1998 as compared with +1.41 in 1997. It is assumed, however, that final demand will recover to 7.35 per cent in 1999. Through an input–output formulation, the sectoral employment level can be estimated. The change in the employment level is –0.66 million persons in the non-agriculture sector in 1998. This is close to the unemployment figure estimated by the NESDB and adjusted by the open unemployed who are seeking jobs (who do not want to be unemployed) and waiting for agricultural seasonally employed which are on average 0.6 million persons.

Other aspects of the impact from the financial and economic crisis are what has happened to the absorption capacity of the informal sector in Thailand, deterioration of the wage level owing to wage cuts, retrenchment and training referral, female-labour force discrimination in lay-offs, the role of the labour union in lay-offs and so on are not clear at the moment.

Table 3.5   Change in employment under the economic crisis, 1996–99

Unit: Persons

Sector	1996/97	1997/98	1998/99
Mining	–200	562	2 984
Manufacture	–81 086	131 403	386 090
Utilities	–213	–3 764	7 501
Construction	–151 203	–207 392	61 857
Trades	–147 143	–135 398	111 937
Transport and Communication	9 019	–25 111	29 364
Banking and Finance and Other services	292 505	–50 541	105 226
Business Services	471 104	–376 120	128 924
Sub-Total	392 783	–666 360	833 884

Notes: Mining = code 012 014; Construction = code 047–048;
Banking and Finance = code 050 053–055 057
Manufacture = code 015–044 ; Trade = code 049;
Business Services = code 056
Utilities = code 045–046; Transport and Communications = code 051–052
Source: Table A1 in Appendix

3.2   Impact on education and health

The social impact on the education and health sectors can be summarized as follows: 1) increased dropouts from the school system as parents are laid off, especially in the poor households; 2) reduced budget for the education sector due to government budget cut; 3) private schools and universities are facing financial difficulties as the ability households to pay decreases and government budget is cut.

In the health sector the impact is as follows: 1) increasing pressure on the low-income households to access health services since their ability to pay decreases; 2) increasing costs of health care to the households, especially the poor households; 3) private hospitals face a declining demand and high costs of provision, while public hospitals face a diminishing budget and cashflow problems as the poor cannot pay for full medical costs. Many private hospitals facing financial distress may terminate their services. The public medical providers will face untenable rising demand.

4. Economic reform under the IMF and its impact on the real sector

4.1 High interest rate policy and tight monetary controls

The Thai government is trying to solve the financial crisis along the advice of the IMF as spelt out in the Letter of Intent. In the immediate future, the government has to exercise a drastic reform of the financial system as well as to revise the macroeconomic framework after an assessment of the real situation. Under the austerity policy and tight monetary controls, the high interest rate policy was the main instrument. Private investment and consumption have declined more sharply than expected.

The tight monetary situation has happened since August 1997 and this has led to increases in the minimum retail lending rate (MRR) in September, October and December 1997 as the deposit rate for one year has not changed at 10–11.5 per cent. The tight monetary situation was reflected by the interbank rate which was 23.87 per cent in September 1997. The minimum lending rate was 15.25 per cent in December while the interbank rate was 21.73 per cent in December 1997.

The BOT has tried to maintain high interest rates in order to restore exchange rate stability. The tight monetary policy has put a severe pressure on domestic demand, the R/P rate in the repurchase market has been set at a level which seems to be higher than the level which the IMF has recommended. The tight monetary policy was received unfavourably by the private sector and resulted in *massive lay-offs and unemployment.* As a matter of fact, the high R/P rate has induced the commercial banks to mobilize their funds to gain the interest rate differential by depositing them with the BOT and lending to the FIDF. In other words, there is no incentive to extend credits to the private businesses which are seriously in need of working capital. Finally, the BOT has reconsidered to decrease the R/P rate from 26 per cent on 20 January 1998 to the level of 20–21 per cent per annum, and during the first week of May 1998 the R/P rate adjusted downwards to 17 per cent for one-day rates, 15.75 per cent for seven-day rates, 16 per cent for fourteen-day and one-month rates, and 16.5 per cent for three-month rates respectively. The interbank rate thus declined from 25 per cent in January to 19.75 per cent in April and 13 per cent in May 1998. Despite the downward interest rate adjustment, the rate is still very high and does not have a stimulating effect on domestic demand so far. It still reflects an 'inverted yield curve effect' or market distortion which still exists as the short-term rates are higher than the long-term rate. The high interest rate policy together with tight liquidity has adverse effects on private consumption, investment and production. It is believed that economic downswings in the case of Thailand as a result of the IMF's prescriptions will be deeper than primarily estimated. The growth rate may be lower than –3.5 per cent per annum This will result in production shutdowns and massive lay-offs in the coming months. Economic recovery may not be feasibly as quick as the IMF has proclaimed.

Furthermore, it is estimated by the Cathay Capital Research (May 1998) that capital outflow over the next 12 months will be not less than $US 14.1 billion. It comprises $US 6.1 billion as repayment of short-term offshore debts that came due at the end of March, $US 8 billion would be needed to repay the BOT's swap obligations.

4.2   Abolition of the two-tier foreign exchange system

On 30 January 1998 the BOT announced cancellation of the system of two-tier foreign exchanges. The 'On-Shore' and the 'Off-Shore' markets of foreign exchange have been in operation since May 1997. As a result, the baht was not overshooting as expected, rather it became stronger. On 2 February the baht was floating in the range of 50.90–51.30 baht per US dollar. It was expected that the baht

Table 3.6   Interest rates, exchange rate and volatility

Month	Interbank (per cent)	Minimum loan rate	Repurchase market rate	Exchange rate (Baht / US$US)	Volatility ratio
Oct-97	18.72	14.63	19.25	37.55	1.37
Nov-97	19.99	14.63	16.5	39.30	0.84
Dec-97	21.73	15.27	20.5	45.29	2.53
Jan-98	21.51	15.25	25.0	53.71	2.1
Feb-98	19.83	15.5	20.25	46.30	2.38
Mar-98	20.57	15.25	21.5	4125	2.44
April-98	19.63	15.25	19.75	39.56	0.63

Note: Volatility ratios expressed by standard deviation of daily spot exchange rate
Source: Bank of Thailand

would be stabilized after this at least until the end of March when another round of loan repayments of $US 31 billion plus a certain amount of swap loss submission were materialized. In fact, the baht did not overshoot since Thailand could manage to borrow another assisting fund from the ADB and the World Bank, and further debts rolled over were agreed by the creditors, especially for loans borrowed by the Japanese companies, for another few months. From Table 1 it is clear that the volatility of exchange rates declined in April 1998. In May 1988 the volatility was still a test case of whether the Thai currency could stand the currency fluctuations in the region or not.

Here, in order to prevent another attack on the currency, the BOT has enforced a ceiling on the non-business transactions in acquisition of the local currency. The ceiling of 50 million baht or roughly a million US dollars was set as an upper bound for the non-resident baht account.

4.3   Financial sector restructuring

The financial sector reform aims to strengthen Thai financial institutions' liquidity and capital adequacy, by normalizing credit flows and bringing down interest rates, to lay a foundation for sustainable economic recovery. The FIDF has intervened in four severely undercapitalized banks (with a deposit share of about 10 per cent) by replacing their management, writing down (virtually fully) the capital of existing shareholders, and recapitalizing them through debt-equity conversion by the FIDF. At the same time, the capital base of the remaining domestic financial institutions, and particularly the core banking system, have been strengthened. It remains imperative to strengthen the legal and judicial framework for foreclosure and bankruptcy. In strengthening the core financial system, the strategy is to strengthen progressively the capital base of all remaining domestic financial institutions through a combination of more realistic loan loss provision and private sector-led recapitalization.

The government would need to restructure the liabilities of the FIDF into government-guaranteed bonds with medium- and long-term maturities and lower interest rates. The imputed interest costs of financial sector restructuring, including loans and equity provided by the FIDF and the costs incurred in setting up the RAB and the AMC, are ultimately fiscal costs that will have to be incorporated into the central government budget. The incorporation of the interest costs of the FIDF's debt into the budget began with the fiscal year 1998/99. The entire debt (net of recoveries) will be serviced by the budget by about the year 2000. Amortization of principal is expected to be met, in part, by privatization receipts.

The government took some additional revenue measures that would allow it to raise tax revenue by about 1/4 per cent of GDP in 1997/98 (1/2 per cent of GDP on a full-year basis). At the same time, the net savings of about 1/4 per cent of GDP could be raised after cutting lesser-priority investment projects while raising spending on the social safety net programme. The net result of these initiatives would be to limit the projected central government deficit to 1.5 per cent of GDP in 1997/98, partly financed by foreign financing and the remainder through modest domestic financing.

In recognition of the adverse economic conditions, the state enterprises were allowed to be slightly in deficit (of 1.5 per cent of GDP) in 1997/98, which was necessary to allow the full drawdown on priority projects financed by foreign creditors, including the World Bank, the ADB and the OECF. The small deficit was financed by foreign sources and raising prices for goods and services provided by state enterprises, except in the specified cases where the move would hurt the poorest members of society (e.g., bus and rail fares). At the same time, further cuts have been made in the investment budget of the largest state enterprises.

Overall, the consolidated public sector deficit was targeted at about 2 per cent of GDP in 1997/98. This excluded the costs of financial sector restructuring, which are being monitored separately and whose interest costs will be brought fully into the budget in the coming years.

4.4   Corporate restructuring and legal reform

The urgent condition for corporate and financial sector restructuring is the international legal framework. In particular, the bankruptcy and foreclosure laws will be amended shortly, in line with the recommendations of technical assistance provided by the World Bank and IMF legal experts. The new Bankruptcy Law will permit corporate reorganizations (as opposed to liquidations), increase the scope for out-of-court workouts (by repealing Section 94(2) of the

Bankruptcy Act) and ensure fair treatment of creditors. Early administrative steps were also being taken to allow foreclosure, with comprehensive amendments of the laws relating to foreclosures proposed for enactment late in 1998. Two other Acts are the Currency Act, including amendments of the Alien Business Law.

4.5 State enterprise privatization

The government has directed the privatization of state enterprises by creating a monitoring system to increase private shares in state enterprises activities. In addition, it has set up a three-year plan to privatize the state enterprises in accordance with the recommendation of the IMF. In the short run, the action plan in the privatization of *energy, transportation and telecommunications* and other infrastructure was drafted in June 1998. Privatization of the Thai Airways International and Bangchak Refinery was achieved by decreasing government's equity share to less than 93 per cent and 50 per cent respectively in line with the IMF recommendation.

The implementation of privatization in the energy sector has not been opposed by the association of public enterprises in principle. However, the process of privatization is still in doubt. The government has been accused, because it was forced by the IMF's agreement to liquidize profitable electricity generating units, being in contradiction of the efficiency criterion of privatization.

5. Government policy to counter adverse social impact

For fear of a severe adverse social impact on employment, education and health, as a result of the austerity measures imposed by the implementing programmes, the Thai government has asked for additional assistance from the ADB and the World Bank (IBRD) in addition to the IMF stand-by credit arrangement. An additional loan from the World Bank of $US 1500 million for the sake of structural adjustments in 3 years (1997–1999) as an *on-going project basis*, while additional loans from the ADB of $US 1200 million were agreed upon. The World Bank has approved $US 300 million in the pipeline for the remedy of social problems as a result of lay-offs and unemployment.

As a medium-term measure, the government has set targets to enforce a repatriation of some undocumented labourers from the

Table 3.7   Thailand's macroeconomic framework, 1996–98

	1996	1997		1998	
	Revised	First review	Estimate review	First	Estimate
Real GDP growth (per cent)	5.5	0.6	–0.4	0–1	–3 to–3.5
Consumption	6.7	0.5	0.1	–1.1	–5.0
Gross fixed investment	6.0	–13.3	–16.0	–6.5	–21.0
CPI inflation (end-period, per cent)	4.8	10.0	7.7	6.0	10.6
CPI inflation (period average per cent)	5.9	6.0	5.6	10.0	11.6
Savings and investment (per cent of GDP)					
Gross domestic investment	41.7	35.8	35.0	34.3	29.1
Private, including stocks	31.5	25.3	23.5	24.7	17.6
Public	10.2	10.5	11.5	9.6	11.5
Gross national savings	33.7	31.8	32.9	32.5	33.0
Private, including stocks	20.6	21.3	22.2	21.7	23.0
Public	13.1	10.6	10.7	10.8	10.0
Foreign savings	8.1	3.9	2.2	1.8	–3.9
Fiscal account (per cent of GDP)					
Central government balance	2.4	–0.9	–1.0	1.0	–1.6
Revenue and grants	19.4	17.6	18.1	16.6	15.8
Expenditure and net lending	17.0	18.5	19.1	15.6	17.4
Overall public sector balance	2.7	–1.5	–1.5	1.0	–2.0
Monetary accounts (end period, per cent)					
M2A growth	12.7	1.5	3.1	6.8	5.1
Reserve money growth	12.0	4.4	4.7	6.8	6.6
Balance of Payment (US$ billion)					
Exports, f.o.b.	54.7	56.4	56.6	60.9	60.1
Growth rate	–1.3	3.2	3.5	7.9	6.2
Import, c.i.f.	70.8	64.2	61.5	64.3	56.8
Growth rate	1.8	–9.3	–13.1	0.2	–7.7
Current account balance	–14.4	–6.4	–3.3	–2.5	4.4
per cent of GDP	–7.9	–3.9	–2.2	–1.8	3.9

Table 3.7   Continued

	1996	1997		1998	
	Revised	First review	Estimate review	First	Estimate
Real GDP growth (per cent)	5.5	0.6	−0.4	0–1	−3 to−3.5
Capital account balance	18.0	−17.9	−18.0	0.3	−12.0 to −14.0
Medium and long-term	12.2	6.5	6.8	8.5	2–3
Short-term	5.8	−24.4	−24.8	−8.2	−15.0 to −16.0
Overall balance	2.2	−24.6	−19.8	−2.2	−8.0 to 10.0
Gross official reserves target	38.7	23.0	27.0	24.8	23.0 −25.0
Months of imports	6.6	4.3	5.3	4.6	4.9–5.3
per cent of short-term external debt	103.0	75.0	93.0	87.0	109–118
Forward position of BoT (end year)	−4.9	−18.0	−18.0	−9.0	−9.0
External debt (per cent of GDP)	48.9	58.6	59.9	76.4	76.3
Total debt (US$ billion)	90.6	94.9	91.7	102.5	85.9
Public sector	16.9	27.8	24.9	35.4	31.7
Private sector	73.7	67.1	66.8	67.1	54.2
Medium and long-term	36.1	38.0	38.2	39.0	33.6
Short-term	37.6	29.1	28.6	28.1	20.6
Debt service ratio	12.3	15.0	15.2	16.8	18.8

Sources: Bank of Thailand Ministry of Finance, International Monetary Fund

neighbouring countries except those who are properly documented and day labourers in the provinces along the borders. It aims to substitute these labourers with domestic labourers who are currently unemployed. Together with this, the Cabinet decided on 27 January 1998 to disburse an ADB assistance fund of $US 300 million to help set up a Center for Assistance to Laid-Off Workers (CALOW) as well as other social development programmes.

In April 1998 the NESDB proposed a $US 480 million loan for a social programme to the Cabinet. The three priority areas that the loan

Table 3.8   Financial reform on banks and remaining finance companies

Measure	Date
1. Prepare restructuring and privatization strategy for the recently intervened banks	30 June 1998
2. Review progress in implementing recently issued MOUs with under-capitalized banks and finance companies	30 April 1998
3. Further strengthen loan classification and provisioning rules so as to bring these in line with international standards by the end of year 2000 and consider their early implementation:	31 March 1998
• present proposal to market participants for comments; and	(performance criterion)
• issue guidelines, including a phased timetable for implementation	
4. Sign new MOUs with all financial institutions of recapitalization plans until the end of 1998 to meet the phased timetable for implementing the stricter rules on loan classification and provisioning requirements:	15 August 1998
• All domestic bank; and	(performance criterion)
• finance companies	15 September 1998
5. Review FIDF policies and operations:	
• establish new FIDF policy framework	30 April 1998
• begin issuance of government-guaranteed long-term bonds; and	30 April 1998
• fully fiscalize FIDF interest costs through issuance of government bonds	By 2000
6. Amend Bankruptcy Law and take initial steps to begin foreclosures and judicial procedures.	31 March, 1998
7. Completion of amendments of laws related to foreclosures	31 October 1998
8. Review of legal framework for banking and supervision with assistance from World Bank/IMF	30 June 1998
9. Issue new prudential regulations including on lending to related parties and foreign exchange exposure	31 December 1998

Table 3.8   Continued

Measure	Date
9. Issue new prudential regulations including on lending to related parties and foreign exchange exposure	31 December 1998
10. Strengthen disclosure requirements, auditing requirements, and accounting practices	31 December 1998
11. Finalize plan for introduction for deposit insurance scheme to replace the current blanket guarantee in the medium term	31 December 1998

Sources: Ministry of Finance and IMF

were targeted for were labour, education and public health. The social programme's target group were the two million unemployed estimated by the Ministry of Labour and Social Welfare, the Interior Ministry and other ministries, especially in the North and Northeastern regions. Projects to be supported included job-creation schemes such as the construction of small-scale reservoirs and channel improvement works. The loan was also allocated to tourism activities.

The World Bank (WB), the Overseas Economic Cooperation Fund (OECF) and the United Nation Development Program (UNDP) were the main sources of assistance in combining with self-finances by the Royal Thai Government to assist in the social project plan. Here, about $US 295 million were allocated to agriculture, public health, labour, industry and interior ministries, the Bangkok Metropolitan Administration and the Tourism Authority of Thailand. The Government Savings Bank would manage another $US 185 million which would be allocated through two main channels: the NESDB's Regional Urban Development Fund project (RUDF) and the Social Investment Fund (SIF). The budget allocated through these two channels would be managed under a new method known as the 'bottom up' system. The new system would not allocate fund from the top down as has been the case in the past but would grant money for any project which aims to strengthen community organizations.

The Social Investment Fund (SIF) is aiming at projects initiated by local community organizations such as the Tambon Administration

Organization (TAO), municipalities, and other unofficial groups such as cooperatives, women's groups, environmental groups or groups associated with temples or schools. Projects under the SIF should be those representing the theme of promoting the formation of a 'civil society' all over the country at different levels. Meanwhile, the Government Saving Bank's Regional Urban Development Fund will act as a loan agency for municipalities nationwide for infrastructure projects, especially those concerning environmental protection. The rest of the loan would be used for *programme operations and as foreign currency reserves*. The Cabinet decided to push forward a social remedy action plan in May 1998. It intended to spend on social investment from the fiscal year 1998/99 budget of 16 000 million baht. The government intended to spend $US 300 million from the WB and $US 100 million from the OECF to add up to its own budget for social programmes. Furthermore, in 1999/2000, the government plans to allocate 5000 million baht from the central budget for solving adverse social impact. The social programmes to be disbursed by this budget are training programmes for unemployed workers, students from the 0.75 million persons who are supposed to be new entrants to be ready for the next recruitment required by the labour market when the economy recovers. In May 1998 the government decided to extend further the privileges from the social insurance policy on medical costs for those unemployed persons. It has actually been extended already for another 6 months.

5.1   Counter measures to lay-offs and unemployment

Under the Cabinet decision in June 1997, the Ministry of Labour and Social Welfare (MOLSW) set up a Center for Assistance to Laid-Off Workers (CALOW) in July 1997, which would act as 'one-stop' service centres providing training referral, counselling and placement services. The centre's activities are funded by an ADB loan. The centre will collect data and information on lay-offs and unemployment. It will study, analyse and propose measures and remedies to counter the problem. It will cooperate with other departments to help the laid-off workers.

In fact, the economic slowdown was noticed by the previous government in June 1997. It has implemented short- and long-run measures. The *short-run measures* are:

(1) monitoring of labour market information, in which the MOLSW cooperates with other ministries such as the ministries of commerce and industry, the board of investment, and NESDB in order to analyse and evaluate the business situation to obtain an accurate number of possible laid-off workers;
(2) cooperating with employers so that laid-off workers would obtain compensation such as severance payments, wages, etc., according to labour protection laws;
(3) trying to find new placement for unemployed persons;
(4) providing training referral;
(5) consulting with the ministries of agriculture, industry and education and cooperatives, retraining for new occupations and looking for funding sources.

The *long-run measures* are:
(1) promoting private provision of labour skill training;
(2) concentrating in labour skill training in the trade of industrial technicians which are in great demand of more than 397 740 persons a year;
(3) training in servicing skills of housekeepers, drivers, chefs in the hotels;
(4) creation of employment opportunities in the rural areas.

In June 1997 the MOLSW has asked for cooperation from the employers through its 'remedy measures for lay-offs' which has the following detail:

(1) Cost saving on the management side should be done before implementing cost reduction on the labour side. It should be ranked according to the degree of severance effect on the labour side.
(2) Measures on employment reduction must be done after a new recruitment is terminated; if there is any vacancy current workers should be given priority; if workers are transferred from one position to another, it would not aversely affect workers' income and benefit; early retirement must be on a voluntary basis; termination of contract must be prioritized from the latest recruited persons, employees who have unfavourable work records, and work ethics.

In September 1997 the MOLSW had invented a system of reporting on lay-offs and unemployment. This is very close to a labour market information system. At the provincial level, the labour welfare and protection officers would have access to the social welfare officers at the same province to obtain a list of enterprises in which lay-offs occur to verify the number of laid-off employees and assist them to obtain compensation according to labour protection laws. The concluding figures and compensation would be submitted to the provincial governor, director-general, and CALOW on the one hand and reported on the other hand to the Permanent Secretary's Office and the respective labour officers at the provincial level. These employment generation (e.g. information on vacancies, job application forms, training application forms, as well as any new recruitment at the lay-off site), social welfare (e.g. issuance of medical care cards for another 6 months extension), directors of skill development centres (e.g. to recruit for referral training, skill development or new placement training), public welfare (e.g. to provide minimum assistance). For the Bangkok metropolitan level the flow of information would be the, same except now instead of the governor the CALOW would summarize all information and report directly to the higher level. In their report form, the name of the enterprise and the type of business, total number of employees, laid-off numbers, date/month/ year of lay-offs, and the assistance that has been done, such as unpaid wages, compensation and other benefits, would be recorded.

In December 1997 the MOLSW, under a new minister of the new government, drafted an action plan on lay-offs and employment. The main action plans comprised measures to *protect the lay-offs,* and *measures to mitigate unemployment problems.* The measures to protect the lay-offs are:

(1) mitigation of lay-offs by cost-saving on both sides, such as temporary calls off-work on holidays and overtime work, shortened working hours and wage reduction, early retirement;
(2) labour relation measures by transparently explaining the situation to the labour union and every concerned party before implementing the mitigation measure;
(3) enterprises' liquidity problem-solving measures by gathering a list of enterprises and informing the Ministry of Finance and the Bank of Thailand.

The *short-term measures* for mitigation of unemployment are: (1) Thais assist Thais to mitigate on the rising costs of living and minimal lending to assist unemployed persons to find a new way of living to sustain their livelihood, and (2) rural employment which directs every ministry to adjust its budget such that labour intensity will be at least 30 per cent in terms of its wage bill. This is to assist the expected disguised unemployment of 1.2 million plus those 'U-turn' unemployed persons of 0.3 million in 1998. *Medium-term measures* are: (3) Foreign guest labourers will be asked to repatriate with the cooperation of the neighbouring countries. (4) Thai labourers should be promoted to work abroad. (5) Promotion of employment in the industrial sector with various measures to assist in cost saving, marketing promotion, recruit of laid-off persons, skill development for new technology, investment opportunities in agriculture, and promotion of self-employed business. *Long-term measures* are: (6) New development theory according to the idea of His Majesty the King.

The MOLSW has also initiated a new 'National Committee on Remedy of Lay-Offs and Unemployment' chaired by the Prime Minister. In addition, the MOLSW also seeks financial assistance from the World Bank (IBRD) and the ADB for its implementation of plans.

The planned targets of each measure are as follows:

Measure 1: *Rural Employment Generation*

This measure has objectives to (1) mitigate the unemployment problem in the rural area for a short period of one year; (2) try to create additional cash income for rural households to supplement for the loss of jobs. This measure sets a rural employment creation of 320 000 persons as its target within the 9 months' periods.

Measure 2: *Foreign Guest Labour*

This measure sets a target to substitute 300 000 foreign labourers with Thai labour.

Measure 3: *Promotion of Employment in the Industrial Sector*

This measure tries to (1) support export-oriented firms as well as firms with high labour intensity; (2) promote of rural/regional industrial activities to absorb those U-turn unemployed workers; (3) create employment opportunities. The target is set to maintain more than 500 000 employed persons in the sector, while creating job opportunities in the rural area and for these unemployed persons.

Measure 4: *Sending Thai Labour to Work Abroad* The target is set to send at least 210 000 Thai workers abroad.

Measure 5: *Project According to His Majesty the King's New Theory on Agriculture Development*

This project is to help those U-turn unemployed persons who seek to find a new way of living in the rural/agriculture sector, such that their occupation and income are sustainable in the long run. The idea is to balance land use and water resources for agriculture in each particular agricultural household. In 1998 there are 8000 work places to be given to 20 000 unemployed persons.

Measure 6: *Thais Assist Thais*

This measure tries to mitigate the difficulties from the rising costs of living faced by the unemployed: supporting the initiation of new occupations for the general labour and unemployed persons; expanding the scope and marketing channel of the goods market produced by the general labour (the targets of this measure are to distribute cheap necessary products for the general public who are in need); creating community business, training the general people on business, arranging welfare for unemployed households.

Measure 7: *Projects on New Light of Occupation*

This measure coordinates and disseminates information about occupation, skill development, training, and counselling for mental reliefs. The targets are: (1) disseminating information to 120 000 laid-off workers and to new entrants to the labour force from the education system who still cannot find jobs; (2) extending opportunities to enter the graduate level with 3000 more places; (3) training of skills in independent occupation for 7000 persons; (4) hiring

1000 graduates to work for the local administrative bodies; (5) finding job opportunities for 20 000 graduates.

Through the above mentioned measures, it is estimated that 1 137 221 direct jobs will be created, and an indirect employment of 901 072 persons, and in total, there will be 2 038 293 employment places created by these measures. The budget requirements for these measures are roughly 9 000 million baht as direct expenses.

The policy priorities under the agreement with the ADB's assistance are, in short: (1) Support for laid-off workers and the unemployed. As mentioned earlier, the MOLSW has set up the CALOW with branches in the provincial capitals, which will register laid-off workers and provide a one-stop service in the form of training referral, counselling and placement support for both male and female workers equitably. Non-formal education programmes will be developed to support the laid-off workers as well. Social security coverage will be extended for laid-off workers to cover medical care and maternity, disability and death benefits for at least six months after retrenchment. (2) Promoting private sector investment in training through tax reductions, in accordance with the Vocational Training Promotion Act. (3) Improving competitiveness of the labour force by reviewing labour policy in general and minimum wage policy in particular through improving tripartite consultations. (4) Protecting the poor in the informal sector and rural areas. This is consistent with the current movement of the government to push forwards with remedy programmes in 1998/99 and 1999/2000.

6.   Securing the future through sound labour-management relations

The present crisis has several drawbacks for the basic quality of life, social order and social mobility as well as social coalition. There are several civil movements, strikes and protests, etc. However, up to May 1998, the crisis had strengthened the relationship between employers and employees to a large extent. The economic crisis is better accepted by both sides than before. Cooperation through cost-saving in the production process is required before voluntary and random retirements. Firms which house unions play an important role and are doing well in cooperation with the employees. Lay-offs are unavoidable anyhow if the economy is on the verge of a cyclical downswing as in this case. So far, we still do not hear any aggressive movement from either sides of the labour market. On May Day or labour day we observed the cordial relationship between different sections of the community amidst national difficulties.

The amendments to the labour relations act that was implemented in August 1998 may be a new chapter of Thai labour relations. We think that government agencies of concern, either the MOLSW or NESDB, and others are doing their jobs, the employers do not have much alternative either, while the employees themselves have learned the worst lesson in their lifetime.

The crisis should be a lesson for every Thai and make us prepare for the designing of sound labour relations and a safety net to help ourselves in the coming years.

Appendix

Table A3.1   Employment under economic crisis by sector, 1996–99

Unit: persons

	Sector	1996	1997	1998	1999
001	Paddy	9 800 856	10 706 451	11 087 770	12 143 038
002	Maize	244 656	246 101	250 478	279 193
003	Tapioca	507 300	511 826	508 115	546 858
004	Beans and nuts	158 307	160 993	145 805	159 293
005	Vegetables and fruit	1 596 972	1 635 915	1 608 848	1 671 203
006	Sugar cane	766 347	774 974	715 648	752 285
007	Rubber	787 934	798 157	805 269	881 004
008	Other crops	1 185 727	842 386	827 752	883 658
009	Livestock	486 552	450 261	447 988	485 649
010	Forestry	110 971	112 026	102 782	115 371
011	Fishery	481 486	415 933	410 766	431 518
012	Crude oil and coal	6 002	8 885	9 031	9 460
013	Iron ore	11 179	2 708	2 749	3 200
014	Other mining	29 936	35 324	35 699	37 802
015	Slaughter	16 665	21 267	21 196	22 134
016	Food preservation	263 490	276 764	295 270	332 82
017	Rice milling and other milling	87 691	78 509	81 606	89 517
018	Sugar	43 798	42 705	44 600	50 209
019	Other food products	176 350	182 957	183 485	197 927
020	Animal feeds	23 866	19 080	18 724	20 619
021	Beverages	62 753	51 086	49 554	52 607
022	Tobacco	17 554	12 374	12 046	12 615
023	Spinning, weaving, bleaching	234 734	209 887	214 406	223 759
024	Textile products	684 189	644 899	662 624	727 011
025	Paper and Paper products	44 881	60 597	61 741	66 740
026	Printing and publishing	55 998	89 364	89 922	96 531
027	Basic chemicals	2 944	4 573	3 495	4 086
028	Fertilizers and pesticides	113 575	101 818	105 892	125 551
029	Other chemicals	59 728	116 372	168 219	174 600
030	Petroleum refineries	8 620	5 831	5 746	6 027
031	Rubber products	91 575	70 518	75 064	83 699

Table A3.1   Continued

Unit: persons

	Sector	1996	1997	1998	1999
032	Plastic products	51 154	17 204	17 517	19 922
033	Cement and concrete products	92 367	90 245	90 404	92 683
034	Non-metallic products	176 022	169 876	175 961	188 054
035	Ferrous and steel	116 518	130 257	133 722	142 611
036	Non-ferrous metal	110 222	105 382	101 860	117 527
037	Metallic products	177 426	163 319	164 812	179 556
038	Industrial machinery	14 586	18 093	17 972	19 305
039	Electrical machinery and equipment	346 259	365 730	391 118	442 259
040	Production and repair of automobile	442 815	427 955	407 310	422 325
041	Other transport equipment	13 132	11 351	11 741	13 285
042	Leather products	162 664	128 473	134 341	150 806
043	Saw mill and wood products	390 570	360 722	355 782	376 763
044	Other products	252 082	275 932	288 412	319 081
045	Electricity and gas	121 856	118 186	114 493	118 622
046	Water	21 033	24 490	24 419	27 792
047	Building construction	1 996 359	1 811 262	1 621 668	1 676 116
048	Public and other construction	175 621	209 515	191 717	199 126
049	Wholesale and Retail Trade	4 341 523	4 194 380	4 058 982	4 170 919
050	Restaurant and hotels	1 039 442	1 187 700	1 152 103	1 188 35
051	Transportation	903 079	890 940	865 661	890 740
052	Communications	50 695	71 853	72 021	76 306
053	Banking and insurance	258 750	346 151	340 805	350 342

Table A3.1   Continued

	Sector	1996	1997	1998	1999
054	Real estate	36 501	60 593	58 221	62 695
055	Public service and admin- istration	310 679	383 265	382 017	394 464
056	Business services	1 722 144	2 193 248	1 817 128	1 946 052
057	Other services	746 227	706 395	700 418	742 935
058	Unclassified	19 487	9 311	8 212	9 039
001– 011	Agriculture sub-sector	16 127 108	16 655 023	16 911 221	18 349 069
012– 057	Non- agriculture sub-sector	16 105 252	16 498 035	15 831 675	16 665 559
	Total	32 251 847	33 162 369	32 751 108	35 023 667

Note: Calculated through Input-Output formulation Employment = Output* Labour-Output Vector; Output = Leontief Inverse * Final demand. See Final Demand in Appendix Table A3.3.

Table A3.2   Change in employment level 1996–1999

Unit: Persons

	CODE I/O	1996/97	1997/98	1998/99
001	Paddy	905 595	381 319	1 055 268
002	Maize	1 445	4 377	28 715
003	Tapioca	4 526	–3 711	38 743
004	Beans and nuts	2 686	–15 188	13 488
005	Vegetables and fruit	38 943	–27 067	62 354
006	Sugar cane	8 627	–59 326	36 638
007	Rubber	10 223	7 112	75 735
008	Other crops	–343 341	–14 634	55 905
009	Livestock	–36 291	–2 273	37 660
010	Forestry	1 055	–9 244	12 588
011	Fishery	–65 553	–5 167	20 752
012	Crude oil and coal	2 883	146	429
013	Iron ore	–8 471	41	452
014	Other mining	5 388	375	2 104
015	Slaughter	4 602	–71	939
016	Food preservation	13 274	18 506	37 554
017	Rice milling and other milling	–9 182	3 097	7 911
018	Sugar	–1 093	1 895	5 609
019	Other food products	6 607	528	14 441
020	Animal feeds	–4 786	–356	1 895
021	Beverages	–11 667	–1 532	3 052
022	Tobacco	–5 180	–328	569
023	Spinning, weaving, bleaching	–24 847	4 519	9 354
024	Textile products	–39 290	17 725	64 387
025	Paper and paper products	15 716	1 144	4 999
026	Printing and publishing	33 366	558	6 609
027	Basic chemicals	1 629	–1 078	591
028	Fertilizers and pesticides	–11 757	4 074	19 659
029	Other chemicals	56 644	51 847	6 382
030	Petroleum refineries	–2 789	–85	281
031	Rubber products	–21 057	4 546	8 635
032	Plastic products	–33 950	313	2 404
033	Cement and concrete products	–2 122	159	2 279
034	Non-metallic products	–6 146	6 085	12 093
035	Ferrous and steel	13 739	3 465	8 890
036	Non-ferrous metal	–4 840	-3 522	15 667
037	Metallic products	–14 107	1 493	14 744
038	Industrial machinery	3 507	–121	1 333
039	Electrical machinery and equipment	19 471	25 388	51 141

Table A3.2   Continued

Unit: Persons

	CODE I/O	1996/97	1997/98	1998/99
040	Production and repair of automobile	–14 860	–20 645	15 015
041	Other transport equipment	–1 781	390	1 544
042	Leather products	–34 191	5 868	16 464
043	Saw mill and wood products	–29 848	–4 940	20 981
044	Other products	23 850	12 480	30 668
045	Electricity and gas	–3 670	–3 693	4 128
046	Water	3 457	–71	3 373
047	Building construction	–185 097	–189 594	54 448
048	Public construction and other	33 894	–17 798	7 408
049	Wholesale and retail trade	–147 143	–135 398	111 937
050	Restaurant and hotels	148 258	–35 597	36 251
051	Transportation	–12 139	–25 279	25 079
052	Communications	21 158	168	4 285
053	Banking and insurance	87 401	–5 346	9 538
054	Real estate	24 092	–2 372	4 474
055	Public service and administration	72 586	–1 248	12 447
056	Business services	471 104	–376 120	128 924
057	Other services	–39 832	–5 977	42 517
058	Unclassified	–10 176	–1 099	827
001–011	Agriculture sub-sector	527 915	256 198	1 437 848
012–057	Non-agriculture sub-sector	392 783	–666 360	833 884
	Total	910 522	–411 261	2 272 559

Note: Calculated from Appendix Table A1

Appendix Table A3.3   Growth of final demand at constant price of 1988

Year	Government expenditure	Export	Private expenditure	Gross fixed capital formation	Final demand
1991	6.19	15.14	5.42	12.68	9.98
1992	6.40	13.81	8.70	6.64	9.36
1993	5.11	12.74	8.31	9.28	9.63
1994	8.19	14.22	8.12	11.60	10.84
1995	5.63	15.49	7.40	11.17	10.75
1996	9.25	-1.76	6.02	5.72	3.69
1997	6.30	8.00	-2.04	-1.90	1.41
1998	-21.37	9.64	-3.10	-8.80	-1.73
1999	8.00	15.00	3.50	2.00	7.35

Note: in 1998 budget was cut 182 000 million baht. from 936 000 million baht Growth of GDP is assumed to be –3.5 per cent.

Abbreviations

AMC	Asset Management Corporation
BIBF	Bangkok International Banking Facilities
NIEs	Newly Industrialized Countries
IMF	International Monetary Fund
FIDF	Financial Institution Development Fund
FRA	Financial Restructure Agency
NESDB	National Economic and Social Development Board
OECF	Overseas Economic Cooperation Fund
RUDF	Regional Urban Development
SIF	Social Investment Fund
NSO	National Statistical Office
MOLSW	Ministry of Labour and Social Welfare
CALOW	Center for Assistance to Laid-off Workers

References

Brooker Group Ltd (1998), *Impact of Thailand's Economic Crisis on the Social Sector*, A final report prepared for the National Economic and Social Development Board, under Asian Development Bank, T.A. No. 2920, Social Impact Analysis of the Economic Crisis, 13 March 1998.

International Labour Organization (1998), *The Social Impact of the Asian Financial Crisis*, Technical report for discussion at the High-Level Tripartite Meeting on Social Responses to the Financial Crisis in East and South-East Asian Countries, Bangkok, 22–4 April

Kitti Limskul (1997), 'Economic Crisis and Impact on Employment: An Input–Output Analysis' in *Labour by Occupation Survey* (1997), Department of Employment Service, Ministry of Labour and Social Welfare.

Yongyuth Chalamwong, (1998), *International Migration and Labour Markets in Asia*, Thailand Country Report, paper prepared for a conference organized by the Japan Institute of Labour, Tokyo, 29–30 January 1998.

4

Asian Economic Crisis and the Crisis of Analysis: A Critical Analysis through Buddhist Economics

Apichai Puntasen

> *To be a tiger is not that important, the most important thing is that we have sufficiently enough to meet our own needs, and the sufficient economics means a sufficiency for self-supporting*

King Bhumibhol's speech on 4 December 1997

1. Introduction

The Asian economic crisis in Thailand has been analysed by a leading economist in Thailand, Ammar Siamwalla (1998: 1–7), as economic mismanagement by the Bank of Thailand (BOT) starting from its decision to liberalize the financial system, particularly in its relationship to the rest of the world. The first move was to accept the obligations under Article VII of the International Monetary Fund (IMF) in 1990 that requires the lifting of all controls on foreign-exchange transactions on the current account. The second was the opening of the Bangkok International Banking Facility (BIBF) in 1993 which was designed to make Bangkok a centre for financial services by encouraging foreign financial institutions to set up operations in Thailand. As a result, most foreign-exchange control measures were removed. In 1992 all ceilings on interest rates were removed. Weakness did appear in the stock market where control measures against speculation were insufficient, resulting in speculative fever from 1993 to 1995.

One major mistake committed by the BOT was pegging the exchange rate virtually with the US dollar while the monetary system was completely liberalized. With a fixed exchange rate while the domestic rate of interest in the early 1990s was much higher than the rate available in international markets, short-term foreign loans flowed in to take advantage of this differential. Worse still was that most of these short-term loans were used to finance the inflated real estate sector as well as the speculation in the stock markets. Such a serious problem was veiled by a good performance of exports during 1992–1995. Early in 1996 exports started to slow down resulting in part from the appreciation of the US dollar which the baht currency was pegged. The complete halt of export growth in 1996 exposed all the problems. By that time the country had already accumulated foreign debts of $US 80 billion and the majority of them were of short-term nature.

Beginning in November 1996, waves of attacks were made against the baht in hope that the BOT would be forced to devalue the baht. Each wave was met by strong defences by the BOT. The fiercest ever came in May 1997, and by the middle of May the Bank had almost run out its net reserves of $US 33.8 billion. This resulted eventually in the floating of the baht on 2 July 1997 and a series of financial crises took place, as is already well recorded.

Internationally this crisis can be analysed in a slightly different light, even though it can be viewed as a problem of mismanagement on the part of the Thai monetary authorities, since problems of a similar nature can be clearly predicted to have come about eventually. With *economic globalization*, when goods and money are allowed to flow freely anywhere in the world, greed can be further generated without restraint or control, especially by those who control capital (Korten, 1996: 71). Under the condition of integrated economies, those who have capital are bound to be in an advantaged position. When the economies are merged, capital can flow to whichever localities offer maximum opportunities to externalize costs. The basic consequence is to shift costs from investors to the community (Daly and Cobb Jr, 1989: 209–35). Under such a circumstance an economic crisis will eventually take place in the net capital-receiving countries sooner or later, regardless of the performance of the economic management agencies.

Apart from taking advantage of a maximum opportunity to externalize costs, free flows of foreign capital can easily generate economic instability. This is the problem faced by Thailand in the current economic crisis. The internationalization of capital and the internationalization of finance since World War II have turned capital into a foot-loose factor of production in both time and space. The quick mobility of capital from that of low returns to the higher ones to take advantage of speculation in security markets anywhere in the world results in economic instability in the countries where massive amounts of capital move in and out in a short period of time (see Freeman, 1996; and Felix, 1994: 365–94). At the macro level, a country with a sufficient amount of domestic savings will be less affected by such a nature of capital flows. In Asia, Japan, Taiwan and Singapore are cases in point.

Both the adverse economic import of foreign capital taking advantage of external costs, and a quick mobility of capital that can cause economic instability have pointed to the crisis of analysis based on the concept of economic liberalization, with a strong emphasis on quick growth without much consideration of economic stability and long-term sustainability. This is why the Asian centric economics or, in the case of Thailand, Buddhist Economics based on a curtailment of 'greed' need to be closely scrutinized.

2.   Buddhist economics

Buddhist Economics is a new way of understanding economic activities by applying a new paradigm about human nature as discussed in Buddhism since its inception. Not much can be argued against the analytical process of economics as such, since the general rules of logical deduction are as well applied in the subject in recent times as in any other. However, some specific paradigms, especially those concerning human nature adopted in the mainstream economics, have not been sufficiently scrutinized. Most of them have been taken more or less at face value. After that, more sophisticated analyses have been built on a rather soft foundation. As a result, many conclusions derived from the analytical process are not able to stand up to critical challenges. Some of its basic paradigms concerning the nature of human existence adopted in conventional economics do not represent actual human behaviour and some may not be consistent with, or may even be in contradiction to, natural laws. These factors result in a weakening of the explanatory power of the conventional or mainstream economics. Replacing such weak paradigms, the one from Buddhism reflects more truly the nature of human beings, and the proven natural laws mentioned earlier could enhance the explanatory power of the mainstream economics. This is why the modified subject should be called 'Buddhist Economics'. The concept is slightly different from that of 'Economics for a Buddhist' because the latter will not deal squarely with the deficiency in mainstream economics. It merely investigates economics from the point of view of a Buddhist who has certain sets of 'values' and 'beliefs'. It does not attempt to investigate either Buddhism or economics.

Without challenging the existing paradigms in economics, the analytical weakness in mainstream economics will not likely be exposed. 'Buddhist Economics' prepares to take up the challenge by pointing out the fundamental weaknesses that exist in mainstream economics and replacing them with more realistic concepts available in Buddhism, with the hope that better conclusions can be reached, in part, to reduce the crisis of analysis that exists in the current economic crisis in Asia.

3. Division between positive and normative economics as a fundamental weakness

The clear division between positive and normative economics can be regarded as a starting-point for the crisis of analysis in economics. Positive economics is defined as an analytical objectivity or sometimes called 'natural law' without value judgement. The concept is in contrast with normative economics where opinion or value judgement can be incorporated. Such division results from the lack of a coherent understanding of the true nature of human existence.

Positive economics assumes 'greed' or, to put it more mildly, 'self interest' as a cardinal nature of human existence which will direct most of the 'rational behaviour' of human activities. Any law based on this 'fact' is a natural law and hence all economic activities conforming to such laws are positive economics. As a result, utility maximization is considered as rational behaviour and positive economics. According to Jeremy Bentham, each person is essentially a self-serving unit – that all individuals are motivated by desire to do things which serve their own best interest – the desire to seek pleasant experiences and to avoid or escape from painful ones (Bowden, 1990: 77).

One may question further whether the 'law' expounded by Bentham is really a 'natural law' and that it is true in all cases without any exceptions. Should any individual who behaves differently from that be considered an exception to this law or is that person behaving irrationally? One may even ask further if the behaviour of most human beings must be like what Bentham has said. Can there be a different pattern of human behaviour than what is already discussed above? If there are many other different patterns of human behaviour than those the law had already propounded, for example 'people [who] insist on loving their own arch enemies, and the ones who prepare to work hard for the sake of the others and live frugally', should those people be considered to have behaved irrationally or they are just the exception to the general rule or they include their own value judgement into their actions. Or, better still, should people of such nature not have existed in the real world? If such a behaviour of human beings does exist and it is a fact that they are in direct contradiction to the 'true' nature of human existance, then should one consider that positive economics is only positive because it complies with its own rules by its own definition? If so, one may ask how positive is positive economics. Most mainstream economists do not want to face such a difficult question. They prefer to accept the concept at its face value and quickly rush to the mechanistic parts of the discussion at which they find that they are in position to have full control of their own arguments. The only unfortunate part is that a mere mechanistic operation based on a shaky foundation will never result in any firm ground or firm conclusion.

A more refined version of utility but no less ambiguous is the one advocated by Boulding (a) (1968: 193–4):

> Economics clearly recognizes that all material objects are intermediate goods, mere means which serve the end of increasing that ultimate *spiritual product* known technically as 'Utility'. The

economist does not know what utility is, any more than the physicist knows what electricity is, but certainly could not do without it.

Not many economists even contemplate the said definition but rush instead to the mechanistic part shown below.

Mechanistic procedures

Given the above set of positive rules that people will try to get the most for themselves, the (direct) utility function U – the analysis is similar when an indirect utility function is used – of an individual or consumer consuming all of his/her income Y on a basket of n (positive) commodities (X_i, $i = 1,..., n$) is defined as:

$$U = U(X_1, X_2, ... , X_n) = U(X)$$

and with P_i for the price of commodity i , the budget constraint for income Y is defined as:

$$Y = \Sigma P_i X_i$$

The rule to maximize U subject to the budget constraint Y can be carried out first by setting up a Lagrangean function L:

$$L = U(X) - \lambda[Y - \Sigma P_i X_i]$$

and the first-order condition for maximization in this case is:

$$\delta L/\delta X_i = U_i - \lambda P_i = 0$$

or $U_i = \lambda P_i$

and $\delta L/\delta \lambda = Y - \Sigma P_i X_i = 0$

where $U_i = \delta U/\delta X_i$ is the marginal utility with respect to commodity i. Thus:

$$U_i/U_j = P_i/P_j$$

The last result states that the marginal rate of substitution between two commodities is equal to the ratio of their prices. Alternatively, the condition can be rearranged to give:

$$U_1/P_1 = U_2/P_2 = \dots = U_n/P_n = \lambda$$

The Lagrange multiplier λ can be shown to be the rate at which U increases as money income increases:

$$\lambda = dU/dY = U_Y$$

The Lagrange multiplier λ is the marginal utility of money income since U_i/P_i is the rate at which utility increases as more money is spent on commodity i.

Apart from what have been discussed above, the following set of assumptions have also been made in order to derive the above properties of the consumer demand equation:

1. The utility function is continuous and 'smooth'.
2. $\delta U/\delta X_i > 0$, the more commodity consumed the higher is the utility.
3. $\delta U^2/\delta X_i < 0$, the marginal utility increases at a decreasing rate or the diminishing marginal utility prevails.
4. $dU^2 < 0$, the convexity property of the utility function.

These assumptions are made for the convenience of mathematical operation and to satisfy the requirements of rational behaviour. The operation itself is a 'positive' operation or a straightforward one. The assumptions themselves do not necessarily imply any positive rule about the utility function itself. Unfortunately, once the set of assumptions has been overlooked or forgotten, the rule itself has been interpreted as a positive rule.

Observe also that the above rule is very rigid because it is designed to generate a set of well-performed mathematical properties and does not necessarily reflect the situation in the real world. For example, it is impossible to discuss efficiency in consumption based on such specific nature of the utility function. No one can assure with one hundred per cent certainty that the utility function must be continuous and smooth. Last but not least, the assumption of

$\delta U/\delta X_j > 0$ (the more, the better) is only true in an isolated case of each individual commodity. Normally a person's reasoning in acquiring a commodity for consumption is much more complex and the case can never be treated as an isolated one. Unfortunately most mainstream economists prepare to forget the above set of rigid rules and prefer to treat them as a general rule because if they relax the said set of assumptions, the foundation of their basic beliefs will be shaken. As well as trying to avoid being normative in their beliefs, they have made their beliefs a positive rule through mechanistic procedures an action that does not actually contribute to a more solid foundation for their analyses.

Instantaneous nature of the utility function

Observe also from the utility function above. It contains no time element in the function, implying that the function is instantaneous with respect to time. A person will experience enjoyment, happiness, gratification, satisfaction, passion and fascination through the consumption of a commodity or a service only instantaneously. Such a state will decline afterwards. Note also that many terms are introduced to represent a feeling of satisfaction at the time of consumption. None of them carries the meaning of utility because utility is in fact an ambiguous word without any clear meaning, as Boulding has already admitted.

The fact that this utility function involves no time dimension as well as another general rule imposed on this function, that it is not inter-personally comparable, has made the whole concept rather absurd when being confronted with 'scarcity', the only solid foundation for the existence of economics. Under the general condition of scarcity of resources, this utility function implies that it cannot make any value judgement about whether a limited resource should be made available to produce food at a very cheap resource cost, or whether one luxurious car that requires a huge amount of resources should be made: in other words, whether to satisfy either the starving poor or the very rich. Either one of them will obtain an 'instantaneous' satisfaction from consuming food or a luxurious car, respectively. Any layman with common sense will agree without much thinking that the limited resources should be devoted to produce food for the poor rather than to produce a luxurious car. However, if a mainstream economist cannot provide satisfactory answers to this obvious question, one should cast doubt on the logic of their thinking, or question their basic assumptions used in formulating their theories.

The question may rest on pleasure and pain

Jeremy Bentham has suggested that a human being will seek maximum pleasure and avoid pain based on his/her previous experience. The concept is widely accepted in the Western world and is considered a rational behaviour of human existance. However, if the concepts 'pleasure' and 'pain' are replaced by slightly different words but with a vastly different meaning of 'happy' and 'misery or suffering', will there be any significant change in the conclusion? Suppose a statement is advanced in such a way that a human being seeks to maximize happiness and to avoid misery or suffering, would there be any change in the conclusion discussed above? An immediate response would be: what is the meaning of happiness and misery. The two concepts are only available in the East, especially in Buddhism.

In Buddhism, only misery or suffering needs to be defined. It is like a temperature. One only needs to specify the level of heat. With less heat it will be more 'cool'. Similarly, with less misery there will be more happiness. There are different degrees of happiness in Buddhism ranging from sensual indulgence or hedonism (similar concept found in the West) to happiness from 'enlightenment' resulting in 'clear', 'clean' and 'calm'. Therefore in Buddhism to minimize 'misery' is equivalent to maximizing happiness, in the same way that minimizing cost is equivalent to maximizing profit in mainstream economics.

Misery or suffering is defined as a sense of lack or alienation or a state of conflict or contradiction in an individual (Phra Rajvaramuni, 1983: 21). The cardinal conflict of all is that a person conceives there is such a thing called 'self' and tries to hold very tightly on to it, while in reality there is no such a thing. What could be perceived as self is in fact a temporary composition of the 'Five Aggregates' in a specific way, instantaneously. They are: corporeality, feeling or sensation, perception, mental formation or volitional activities, and consciousness (Pha Rajvaramuni, 1983: 15). Without any one of them, a human being will not exist in full. From one second to the next a person will be a completely different one because each element in the composition has already changed. The insistence is on temporary or impermanent composition of the Five Aggregates because another natural law states that everything is impermanent or changing all the time. This has been known as the law of 'impermanence' which is another fundamental law of nature (Phra Rajvaramuni, 1983: 20). Because of the fact that everything is changing, it is better to acknowledge the change and regard everything as impermanent including the one of self. As a person tries to cling or to hold on to his/her self while in fact everything is changing, the result will be conflict or contradiction with the natural law of change or impermanence. Because a person tries to cling to self as if it really exists, the person can easily generate suffering or misery through the three evils, namely, desire or greed, hatred and anger, and delusion. There are the real causes for misery (Phra Rajvaramuni, 1983: 31) .

On the other hand, to be happy is to be clean from desire or greed, to be calm from anger and hatred and to be clear from delusion (Buddadhasa, 1996: 23 and Phra Rajvaramuni, 1983: 28). The utmost act of emancipation for a human being is to be free from the three evils, namely, desire or greed, anger or hatred, and delusion. Where any individual has not yet been emancipated it is because that person does not have the right knowledge (Phra Rajvaramuni, 1983: 31). The most important knowledge among all is the knowledge that there is no such thing as self. As there is no self, one cannot be selfish or greedy (Phra Rajvaramuni, 1983: 32).

According to the Buddhist belief, human existence is at the highest stage of development among all living things. This specific nature gives, a person his/her ability to learn or to develop the Five Aggregates, especially the mental formation and the consciousness, indefinitely (Phra Dharmapidoke, 1993: 34–6). Because of that, human existence can never be too foolish to be developed. The rate of development for each one can be different but all can be developed indefinitely. Due to this important quality of human existence, the only obstacle to a person behaving or reacting differently from what should have been, is ignorance or inadequacy of the appropriate knowledge on the part of that person. If a person has such knowledge, he/she will react differently. As a result, the proper remedy is to generate learning and the most important method in Buddhism is learning through actual experience, through his/her own analytical ability and or through guidance or advice from 'good' friends. Good friends can be a person's parents, teachers, friends and associate, or learned persons who have good intentions towards that person, as well as an appropriate learning environment (Phra Dhebhvethi, 1990: 16–17).

What has been discribed above is a set of fundamental teaching principles in Buddhism. The part that is most relevant for the discussion concerns the concept of maximizing utility, by seeking optimal pleasure and avoiding pain, underlying mainstream economics which is a rather shallow concept that does not touch the inner core of the human being. The concept that a human being should liberate him/herself from misery in order to attain 'permanent' happiness, in the author's opinion, is a much more superior concept. The cause of misery most relevant to economics is desire or greed due to ignorance or delusion. The concept of happiness in Buddhism discussed here does not match the one in the West that normally carries the range of meanings discussed earlier, such as enjoyment, gratification, satisfaction, passion or fascination. No wonder that the concept of efficiency in consumption cannot be adequately treated in mainstream economics.

4.   Efficiency in consumption explained in Buddhist economics

There are actually two levels of misery in Buddhism. First-degree misery is more or less a physical problem caused by a deprivation from basic essential needs, namely, food, clothes, shelter and medicine. A person will suffer severely when he/she does not have an adequate amount of food and nutrients to maintain his/her faculties. It is said in Buddhism that the misery from having inadequate food is the worst misery of all, since a person will have no way of organizing him/herself (not to mention to develop their mind) when starving (Phra Dharmapidoke, 1998: 6). It is the greatest misery or contradiction of all as the body cannot properly function. Deprivation of medicine, clothes and shelter respectively is less severe. Such misery caused by physical deprivation can only be eased by providing what a person needs. There is no other way to get round this problem. The needs must be satisfied. These needs are known as essential needs.

However, for this second-degree misery, just discussed, the desire has been propelled by greed resulting from not knowing the natural law that there is no such thing as self. His/her own greed or desire may burn a person inside, if his/her 'artificial' want has not been satisfied (Phra Dhebhvethi, 1990: 79–81). However, a physical part of that person will not be affected by such a deprivation from not being satisfied because it is a separate compartment. Most likely a person will not be killed by the deprivation or the suppression of such desire. Of course, the true remedy is to help the person to realize the existence of the natural law of selflessness by him/herself. To supply a person with what he/she desires will not solve the problem, in fact it will aggravate the problem. Even by applying this case to the utility function of mainstream economics, one will observe that the person will only achieve an instantaneous gratification when the desire is satisfied. The fact that the previous desire has been satisfied, as previous experience shows, only leads to the higher level of desire being spirally stimulated within a person that could result in endless sets of desire. A good mainstream economist will argue that budget or income constraint will serve as a watergate to prevent the flood of such spiralling desire. Unfortunately, for some persons, before the watergate of income constraint is properly closed, a lot of damage has already resulted from resources consumed in producing commodities to satisfy such an unsatiated desire.

It is quite clear from the above discussion that efficiency in consumption is the consumption that satisfies the basic essential needs (first-degree misery) and not to satisfy the demand (even the effective one backed up by income) generated by artificial want (second-degree misery). For the reasons explained earlier, such a question cannot be treated adequately in mainstream economics.

Without a proper treatment of the issue, the discussion of efficiency in production of mainstream economics is only analogous to trying to cut paper with one-bladed scissors. It is not the most effective way to cut paper. In order to bring more sense to the discussion of efficiency in production, efficiency in consumption must be equally and clearly defined. The concept can only be adequately treated by Buddhist economics. The real weakness of mainstream economics is its method of inquiry into human existense in the West which is only skin-deep and not so thorough an analysis as that of Buddhism.

5.   Reasons for different levels of investigation

Mainstream economics, in spite of its claim to be a value-free or positive science, does in fact have its cultural root in the evolution of Western culture with the following set of dominant characteristics:

(1) Self-interest is a normal motive for human beings since it only reflects their true nature;
(2) Individualism, individual rights and freedom as well as property rights are an essential part of human existence they must be protected and should not be infringed;
(3) Family institution is vital for the continuation of human society;
(4) The ability to control nature will improve the quality of life physically;
(5) Technology is the most important tool for the control of nature.

Many hypotheses have been advanced in an attempt to explain cultural roots. Among many convincing arguments, climatic difference seems to offer one plausible explanation. The need to survive through the long cold winter is experienced annually by people in the West. Accumulation of food, fuel and clothes for the whole family to survive the long winter is considered an essential and normal activity. The whole family has more time together during the winter and there is more time to read, write and reflect during that long period of time. Any successful attempt at controlling nature would generally lead to an enhancement of the quality of life. As a result, technology has been invented and developed for this purpose (Phra Dharmapidoke, 1998: 54).

Such a culture is radically different from those in the East where most people live in a tropical climate, though some do, in fact, live in a temperate climate. There has been no pressure on food supply all year round. Sharing food as a method of ensuring food security for the people who live in tropical climates makes those people look more caring and sharing. Since nature has not been so hostile to them, there is no need to control nature but to live in harmony with it. In a tropical climate, people live in a more closely knit community. The communal life receives much more emphasis than that of a family unit or even an individual. As a result, communal ownership in the past was much more important than private ownership.

Under such circumstances, physical difficulty or trouble is not a real problem or real threat to Eastern people. Yet, under such an ideal situation of physical convenience, they are still not fully satisfied. They have, nevertheless, been troubled by inner desires. Investigations into the real cause of the problem must be made beyond the skin-deep stage and deeper into the human soul. The culprits being discovered are the three evils, greed or desire, hatred or anger, and delusion. This is why the treatment for misery or suffering in the East must be done at a different level than that in the West, where the cause of inner suffering has hardly been investigated.

Unfortunately, the sharp contrast between the two cultures (East and West) has been diminished by the emergence of capitalism. At its inception in the West, in the early sixteenth-century dawn of mercantilism, John Calvin had engineered to modify Christianity in order to accommodate the Christian middle class in Europe as well as to facilitate accumulation of capital through his invention of 'Puritan Ethics' (Tawney, 1922: 91–111). A factory process introduced by the industrial revolution in the eighteenth century resulted in mass production. According to Say's law of supply creating its own demand, the mass production provided a big push for industrialists and for businessmen to induce consumption through massive advertising campaigns. As a result, consumption is inevitable. During the whole process of development of the three modern evils, capitalism, industrialism and consumerism, money has its own evolution along the way – from that as a medium of exchange, to a store of value, to capital that can always generate earnings, and recently as a commodity that can be used for speculation. Its form or shape has undergone a significant transformation from that of shell, animal or primitive commodity, to silver, gold, to bank notes or credit cards. The latest evolution of money is an electronic digital figure with its ability to move instantaneously almost everywhere on the face of this globe. Needless to say, the evil four, capitalism, industrialism, consumerism and the continuous evolution of money, contribute to the corruption of the human mind in both the West and the East. The one in the East is more severe, since they are still quite inexperienced, having been exposed to the evil four over a rather short span of time. Unlike of the West, where the evolution has been rather gradual since the early sixteenth century, the East has received the full-blown impact in most cases within the period of only one century.

Therefore, the impact tends to be more severe in the East than in the West and it will continue to cause more damage to the East for quite some time to come in the foreseeable future. The existence of the modern evil four is the major factor responsible for the unification of the two formerly sharply contrasting cultures of the East and the West.

Much more severe than the coalition of the two contrasting cultures is the rapid degeneration and degradation of global resources and environment brought about by the modern evil four. Such degradation has set a limit to our common spaceship, the earth. Such limit has called for the modification of our common culture, if the human race is to survive in the future. This is why the revival of Buddhist economics, in a manner similar to the old Lutheran movement at the dawn of mercantilism, is called for (Tawney, 1922: 73–91).

6.   General application of Buddhist economics

In a way similar in which the strong emergence of capitalism prompted John Calvin to modify Christianity to be able to accommodate changes, especially among the middle class, this time the fact that no known 'new colony' exists on this spaceship earth has called for quick modification of slow-to-react conservative mainstream economics. As already discussed, mainstream economics has no analytical tools to deal effectively with the rapidly changing situation, as its operation is much more mechanistic and its guiding light is a rather old and dubious concept of utilitarian philosophy invented at the time of scarcity in Europe. Although Buddhist teaching is even older, it has become more contemporarily aligned because it was invented at the time of adequacy in the East. We are now living admidst plentiful resources, yet catastrophe is right in front of us. It is a rather new but also a rather strange situation. Because of this specific nature it can be clearly explained why Buddhist economics is the most appropriate tool to deal with the problem now confronting us.

Its analytical tools only require people to be alert to the existence of a natural law concerning the non-existence of self. If this concept is clearly understood, human life could be viewed differently from the perspective of being merely a consumer. The most meaningful thing in life does not have to come from consumption. Appropriate consumption can be done without much destruction of resources and environment. In fact, resources and environment can also be upgraded while a person can live just as happily by being clean, calm and clear, and also be very creative. However, the task begining on this new path of thought is to be awakened to the real nature of human existence (or being enlightened) and the law of nature about self and everything else. The law of change or impermanence and understanding cleared of the delusion generated by mainstream economics within the context of the existence of the four evils, capitalism, industrialism, consumerism and money, must be widely propagated.

Out of the crisis: Buddhist economic way

As already discussed earlier, in Buddhism, to try to satisfy greed as the method for maximizing utility does not lead to maximized happiness or minimized suffering on the part of each individual involved. At the same time, inefficient or wasteful uses of resources and environment are also a consequence. The only way out from this problem is to cultivate *panya* or wisdom or ability for critical analysis. Once a person understands the actual nature of life and understands clearly the concept of non-self, a person will not cling to him/herself. Greed will not be easily stimulated. As a result, the consumption pattern of a person will gradually change to more of the real needs rather than that of artificial want or desire (Phra Dharmapidoke, 1993: 21–2). Thus, the cultivation of *panya* or critical analysis is essential for turning the current crisis in Thailand, as well as in Asia generally, into opportunities. The *panya* cultivated will serve as a potent immunization against the disease spread basically by the foot-loose or by the quick mobility of capital, globally. Such a quick mobility of capital has been the original cause of the crisis activated by greed through rapid growth in the region, a decade before the crisis. Unfortunately, such rapid growth also simultaneously accompanied rapid decay generated by rapid accumulation of waste and rapid destruction of resources in the region.

Clearly a fresh approach to development for Thailand and the Asian region is badly needed after all the nonsense.

Under the new direction of development, King Bhumibhol of Thailand explained in the speech on the eve of his birthday on 4 December 1997:

> a sufficient economy does not necessarily mean that every family must grow their own food and make their own clothes, but the village or the district must sufficiently produce to satisfy their own needs. Items produced more than needed can be traded for the insufficient ones. Nevertheless, trade should not be conducted with the too far away places to save transportation cost (Royal Speech, 1997: 18).

Phra Dharmapidoke (Payut Payuto, 1998: 52–64) has proposed the concept of 'economics of the middle path'. Middle Path is a very crucial concept in Buddhism which literally means 'not taking any extreme position'. It could easily be equated to the 'point of equilibrium' in mainstream economics. According to Phra Dharmapidoke (Payut Payuto), the economics of the middle path implies moderate consumption that will result in optimization of 'quality of life' (maximize happiness or minimize suffering). Such a moderate consumption must be strictly under the condition of non-exploitation of oneself as well as of others. In other words, consumption must not result in adverse effects on the ecosystems.

The concepts advanced by King Bhumibhol and Phra Dharmapidoke (Payut Payuto) serve only as examples of how to apply Buddhist economics for the redirection of the country's development in order to ease out of the current crisis, as well as to preempt any possible economic crisis in the future. Actually, some of the said concepts have already been applied in Thailand for more than a decade, especially by small farmers in the various forms of eco-farming such as forest agriculture, natural farming, mixed farming and integrated farming (Puntasen (a), 1996: 85–91; and Puntasen (b), 1996: 279). The result has turned out to be rather satisfactory. Most of those who practised eco-farming in Thailand a decade ago have received almost no negative impact from the current crisis. In fact, most of them are better off because of the deflation of the baht currency, while the inflation rate does not keep pace with the deflated currency. As a result, their real income increases from the increase in the prices of their produce, while their costs remain unchanged due to the fact that they did not use any imported fertilizers and other related chemical inputs.

Other relevant activities related to curtailing the influence of the current crisis, caused by a rapid mobility of foreign capital, are the increase of savings groups, credit unions and their networks. Such activities began to spread very rapidly only a few years ago. Most groups had a very humble beginning. It began with members of the community being requested to put a very modest sum of money such as 10 baht (about $US 0.25 at the current exchange rate) per family to be saved each month. The emphasis is more on individuals to save the money by themselves. The main purpose has been to urge people to come to group meetings to discuss the problems they have faced as a way of exchanging ideas, as well as finding solutions through the group. By the time that sufficient funds have been accumulated, group members are likely to know each other very well and to have already shared many useful ideas, and many useful investment projects will have already been thoroughly evaluated. Then the money is ready to be lent to a few of the most promising investment projects.

An evaluation

It has been almost without exception that these projects have been very successful. As a result, among the saving groups, especially those in the South, the funds have now accumulated to more than 10 million baht for each group. Some already have funds larger than 50 million baht. It is now estimated that the total amount of funds of all these savings groups and credit unions is more than three billion baht. However, the absolute amount of capital is still very small in comparison with the magnitude of the current crisis, which is estimated to be four trillion baht.

Nevertheless, the potential of these savings groups and their networks is very great. Up to the present time, the record of default debt has been negligible, and the whole operation has been very much cost-effective because it only involves a very small fraction of the total amount of funds and because such operating costs only occur once or twice a month – and the wage or honorarium charged is not as high as that of other commercial operations. The whole system is based on communal trust. Many of the groups begin to provide basic social safety nets to members, such as funeral costs, partial compensation for health care and education costs as well as small amounts of pension for the elders.

One can imagine that with a rapid expansion of such savings groups and their networks, together with the self-sufficient economy at the village or district level suggested by the King, the need to depend on foreign capital in the future will be gradually reduced. However, the practices discussed above must be within the framework of the economics of middle path or Buddhist economics where consumption must be undertaken in such a way that no adverse effect can arise to individual happiness (quality of life) as well as to the eco-systems. This is a fresh approach to the development of a possible solution to reduce the severe impact of the current crisis. The only requirements for this approach are a fresh look at life, a clear understanding of the relevant nature laws and enjoyment of life through wisdom, in a way more consistent with the local laws.

7.   Conclusions

The current economic crisis in Thailand and in Asia can be viewed as an opportunity for a fresh look at a new development approach rather than a threat to the existing and decaying economic system. The crisis has led to the fundamental question of the crisis of analysis in itself. Modern economics that has been facilitated by the four modern evils, namely, capitalism, industrialism, consumerism and the latest development in the form and function of money, has resulted in the stimulation of greed generated by human ignorance, or not knowing about the concepts of non-self and related natural laws.

Within the realm of mainstream economics, such ignorance has been reinforced by the ambiguous concept of utility, which is not well understood by most economists themselves. The concept can be crudely explained as one in which an individual is allowed to enjoy as much consumption of goods and services as can be consumed within that individual's budget constraint. There can be no critique of one or the other person's enjoyment. As such, the concept of efficiency in consumption cannot be meaningfully discussed within the framework of mainstream economics. The concept of resource costs incurred in the production of goods for consumption cannot be validly discussed. Hence, the power of discussion of the overall efficiency concept is greatly reduced as one can only validly discuss efficiency in production.

Buddhist economics can deal with this problem much more effectively through the concept of maximizing happiness or minimizing suffering (instead of maximizing utility) by first defining suffering as a conflict or contradiction with a natural law of change or impermanence, in order to understand that there is no such thing as self or a non-self, another natural law. The concept further leads to the discussion of essential needs, the first-degree suffering which is needed to be cured or satisfied, an artificial want or desire. To try to satisfy the latter will result in more escalation of the desire facilitated by the four modern evils, especially consumerism and money.

The Buddhist method for treatment is to suppress the artificial desire with the awareness that the concept of self is, in fact, an illusion. As artificial desire is reduced, economics of middle path can easily be realized. It will make much more sense, then, to introduce the concept of self-sufficient economy as with some actual applications in Thailand, for instance the cases of eco-farming for small farmers and networks of savings groups.

The current economic crisis in Thailand can be validly analysed as a crisis of mismanagement, especially by the monetary authorities within the existing framework of analysis. However, at the international level with rapid mobility of capital globally, the crisis will definitely take place in one form or another through a massive exploitation of resources from weaker economies and the instability of small economies that are the net receivers of foreign capital. This specific nature of the crisis has posed a serious question of sustainability not only for Thailand but the whole Asian region. For this reason, Asian centric economics must be reconceptualized and propagated.

As it turns out, Buddhist economics appears to provide a much more explicit concept of happiness and suffering than that of utility and can result in a solid discussion of efficiency in consumption that leads to overall efficiency in conjunction with efficiency in production, the usual concept available in mainstream economics. With the new approach, not only can the current crisis be greatly minimized but the long-term sustainability of the economy and its development can also be ensured.

References

Boulding, Kenneth E. (1968) (a), *Beyond Economics; Essay on Society Religion and Ethics*, Ann Arbor, University of Michigan Press.

Boulding, Kenneth E. (1968) (b), 'The Economics of the Coming Spaceship Earth' in Jarrett, Henry (ed.), *Environment Quality in a Growing Economy*, Baltimore, Johns Hopkins University Press.

Bowden, Elbert V. (1990), *Economics in Perspective*, Ohio, Southwestern Publishing.

Daly, Herman E., and Cobb (Jr.) John B. (1989), *For the Common Good: Redirecting the Economy toward Community, the Environment and Sustainable Future*, Boston, Beacon Press.

Felix, David (1994), 'International Capital Mobility and Third World Development: Compatible Marriage Troubles Relationship?', Policy Science, Vol. 27, No. 4.

Freeman, Andrew (1996), 'Turning Digits into Dollars: A survey of Technology in Finance', *The Economist* (26 October and 1 November).

Korten, David. C. (1996), *When Corporations Rule the World*, West Hartford, Kumarian Press and San Francisco, Berett-Kochler Publishers, Inc.

Puntasen, Apichai (1996), (a), 'Agro-Industry and Self-Reliance Strategies in Village Thailand', Hoadley Mason C. and Gunnarsson Christer A. (eds), *The Village Concept in the Transition of Rural Southeast Asia*, Richmond, Curzon Press Ltd.

Puntasen, Apichai (1996), (b), 'An Institutional Approach for Environment Protection through Analysis of Incentives: A Case Study of Forests in Thailand', in Kojimer Reeitsu, Nisihara Sigeki, Otsuka Kenji, and Fujisaki Shigeaki (eds), *Environmental Awareness in Developing Countries: The Case of China and Thailand*, Institute of Developing Economics, Tokyo.

Siamwalla, Ammar and Sobchockchai, Orapin (1998), 'Responding to the Thai Economic Crisis'. A paper prepared for the United Nations Development Programme (UNDP, Bangkok). Presented at the High-Level Consultative Meeting, *Policy Response to the Economic Crisis and Social Impact in Thailand*, 22 May 1998, Bangkok, Thailand.

Smith, Adam (1937), *An Inquiry into the Nature and Causes of the Wealth of Nations*, New York, Modern Library.

Tawney, R. H. (1922), *Religion and the Rise of Capitalism: A Historical Study*, New York, A Mentor Book, Published by the New American Library (in Thai).

Buddadhas, Intaphanyo (1996), *Emptiness: Non-self is Emptiness*, Bangkok, Laikanok Press.

Phra Dharmapidoke (Payut Payuto) (1990), *Economics for a Buddhist*, Bangkok, Buddadharma Foundation.

Phra Dharmapidoke (Payut Payuto) (1993), *How to Develop Human Being (Buddhism and Human Development)*, Bangkok, Buddadharma Foundation.

Phra Dharmapidoke (Payut Payuto) (1998), *Observing America to Solve Problems in Thailand,* Bangkok, Buddadharma Foundation.

Phra Dhebhvethi (Payut Payuto) (1990), *Method of Thinking According to Buddhist Dharma*, Bangkok, Panya Press.

Phra Rajvaramuni (Payut Payuto) (1983), *Buddhist Dharma Natural Law and Value for Life*, Bangkok, Mental Health Press.

The Royal Speech (1998), *Handbook for Making living of the People in 1998 and the New Theory*, 4 December Bangkok, Office of the Crown Property, The Mongkol Chaipattana Company, and Bang-chak Petroleums Ltd (Public Company).

5
Asian Economic Crisis and the Crisis of Analysis: Western, Asian and Buddhist Economics

Tran Van Hoa

1. Introduction

In his analysis, Professor Apichai Puntasen, a noted economist from Thammasat University, has presented what he regards as the main cause of the Asian economic and financial crisis which emerged in July 1997 in Thailand, and provided a set of simple but cost- and outcome-effective solutions to minimize its impact and to get the country back to the path of economic development, social stability and individual happiness or satisfaction. Some examples of how the solutions have been successfully used at the village level in Thailand are also given. The idea of reducing wants and needs to reduce problems is based on the traditional tenet of the centuries-old Buddhism but its application is a remarkably refreshing one with immediate practicality in policy and implementation, especially in Asian tropical countries such as Thailand, in modern times. Some comments are necessary for discussion however.

2. Western economics and its axioms

While it is true that, in the classical marginalism-based analysis of economic activities or human endeavours, the axioms of human behaviour are required both mathematically and conceptually for a proper analysis of not only utility but also costs, production, trade, social welfare and international economic relations, this approach is not unique to economics but is applicable to all other social, physical and metaphysical sciences as well. An example often cited for abstract analysis but with practical applications is: While the earth is not flat according to the evidence in modern times, it can, for some practical problems or for a very localized problem spatially (e.g. a house or building), be regarded as flat for convenience of analysis and operation. This approach is necessary especially if this kind of assumption does not change the conclusions (e.g. a house with sound operational and aesthetic characteristics) in any meaningful way. Another example is: While nobody has been able to define what a point (in space) is except in a tautological manner, all of the most practical applications (e.g. a bridge, a house or a temple) in the world that depend on lines (a sequence of points) and space (a group of constituent lines in different directions) are simply based on this concept of a point initially.

The real question here is whether our assumptions are reasonable representations of human behaviour or activities for the individual or, using further assumptions to manage an extension of the issue in a useful way (one such extension issue is the aggregation bias problem), for a cohort of many individuals. The fact that restricted assumptions are sometimes made in order to facilitate the subsequent analysis, reflects the limitations on us as human beings, the limitations of our existing knowledge or state of the art, or the limitations of the technical means of operation. An interesting example in this case is the basic assumptions made in order to derive the best, linear and unbiased (BLU) properties of the Gauss Markov Theorem or the ordinary least squares and maximum likelihood estimation and forecasting method in linear regression analysis. After the reference standard (the BLU properties) has been derived for our regression model, for example, and the estimated model is used as a preferred reference model, our assumptions used in deriving this standard can then be relaxed and our method modified if necessary to accommodate other more realistic situations (e.g. human mistakes are temporally correlated, or different individuals behave differently, or our measurement of happiness may be fuzzy at best) in practice.

3.   Current issues in Western economics

How them do we deal with dynamic and intertemporal issues in utility which Puntasen regards as important but neglected issues in economics? We note that these issues belong to a group of extensions of the standard utility analysis which is initially designed for a representative consumer (or producer in production studies). Among the well-known extensions are aggregation over many individuals (an interpersonal problem), multi-commodity interdependence, intertemporal, and international problems. In the case of dynamic utility, we can regard it as an additive sum of static utilities over time, in a way similar to the concept of a long-run cost curve being the sum of short-run cost curves or to the concept that lifelong experience is the sum of everyday experiences. The properties of a multi-commodity consumption should obey the same rules of consumer-demand behaviour as those for one-commodity cases with the addition of the complementarity or substitution effects. Intertemporal utility has been studied by many economists in the past twenty years or so but, due to its mathematical intractability or complexity, a separable and additive form for intertemporal utility has often been used in formal analysis. Studies of the international (multi-country) kind should follow a logical extension of the multi-commodity and multi-person analysis discussed above.

A methodology is, properly speaking, neutral and general in its formulation and applications. Maximizing a utility is a concept of mathematical and logical (or Boolean) operations, it does not support a particular form or a specific content of the utility function. If we define our utility as essential or primary needs, then that is what it is. If we define our utility as including 'artificial' wants or luxuries which most people in a society can do without, then that is what it is. The method of achieving both stated objectives the best way we can is the same.

A formal way to explain this issue can be through the duality analysis of consumption and production in modern economics. Let us focus only on consumption for convenience. The extension to production is straightforward.

Suppose that in our previous formulation of utility analysis we concentrate on minimizing the costs incurred in achieving a certain set of needs or wants, say U^*. Minimizing costs now can be regarded as a situation in which waste on using resources or finance to attain U^* is at a minimum. This set of needs or wants can be enumerated in an expenditure function (that is, $\Sigma\ P_iX_i$) and how to achieve them at minimum costs is concisely defined as:

Minimize $\quad \Sigma\, P_i X_i \qquad$ subject to:

(1) $U^* (X_1, X_2, \dots , X_n) \geq U^* \qquad$ One must get satisfaction from spending on a commodity

(2) X_i (for $i = 1, \dots , n$) $\geq 0 \qquad$ A commodity must exist

Then using μ for the new Lagrangean multiplier, the problem of how to attain U^* can now be expressed as a Lagrangean function L^* where:

$$L^* = \Sigma\, P_i X_i + \mu\, [\, U^* - U^*(X_1, X_2, \dots , X_n)]$$

and the necessary condition for attaining a minimum L^* is:

$$\partial L / \partial X_i = P_i - \mu\, U^*_i = 0$$

or $\qquad P_i = \mu\, U^*_1$

and $\qquad \partial L / \partial\, \mu = U^* - U^*(X_1, X_2, \dots , X_n) = 0$

Then, we have immediately:

$$U^*_i / P_i = U^*_j / P_j \qquad \text{or} \qquad U^*_i / U^*_j = P_i / P_j$$

The results for minimizing costs or expenditure to attain a certain utility are identical to those obtained earlier for maximizing utility given a budget constraint. Thus, there is a set of rules for minimizing the costs of attaining the pre-specified needs and wants. This set is the same as that obtained by using a given amount of resources or money to attain the most needs or satisfaction.

4.   Buddhist and Asian economics

Puntasen's analysis is useful in pointing out the need to be thrifty in our demand on nature and existing resources, to maintain and, more importantly, sustain a reasonable standard of living for as long our society exists. This living standard is defined by the people in the community and by the evolution of the species. Thus the needs of the bronze-age people are different from those of the twentieth century where the world has been enlightened by the industrial revolution, first in 1850 by the universalization of popular education and by enforcing equality of gender, and then through the advance of information technology in the past 50 years. As noted by an eminent Aborigine in Australia some years ago: While the aborigines had lived in perfect harmony with nature and the environment in Australia for 40 000 years (an ideal situation in sustainable living and development by any standard) by getting only what they needed from the land without destroying it at the same time, they now do not think it is a good idea to walk long distances, to carry heavy weights on their back, to live unclothed in caves or to work in hot offices without air conditioning or fully in the sun without protection against skin cancer or pain.

His analysis is also useful for encouraging people to try to be self-sufficient, for if self sufficient or living within their means, they can survive without much need for external, regional or international transactions. But this is different from isolationism, as isolationism goes against the concept and practice of international human, economic and political relations. And the world community has well learned from its long Darwinian history that it has created a better world, from the beginning of mankind, for the benefit of everyone on earth by hard work, by creative thinking, by learning through doing, by recording experience, by better uses of natural resources and by internationalizing its acquired knowledge, religiously, politically, socially, economically and culturally.

Another pertinent question raised by Puntasen is that the results of classical economics and marginalism analysis, which form the basis for the current concept of economic globalization or its subsets of regional economic integration, can have their market failures or other failings in practical applications. Thus, perfect mobility of the factors of production (including capital and labour) in a national or international market is one of the fundamental assumptions of classical economics, but when short-term capital can be transferred around the world in nanoseconds, without consideration for its impact on the structure or nature of investment that capital has been used for, then we are creating serious problems. Even the most prominent of contemporary financial capitalists or fund managers, George Soros, claimed recently that in the face of the current financial and economic turmoil, controls should be placed on capital movements even in the case of economic and financial globalization. In this context, Puntasen's analysis is useful in pointing out the wisdom of wise business decisions, sound long-term corporate planning strategies with prudential controls and supervision of finance.

Our analysis above appears to indicate that the modern methodology of economic analysis should not be blamed for the economic crises in Latin America in the early 1990s, in major East Asian countries in 1997 and currently in Russia and probably Japan. This methodology, with its universal applicability, can be blended in with local or national issues and objectives (social utility) which are expressed implicitly or explicitly in social and national agendas of the country in question, and it can and should be optimally attained, that is, attained the best way we can. In this form, Buddhist economics is economics with a more severe constraint on individual or social utility for religious, economic or social reasons, and Japanese-style economics or systems are simply those areas of economics with an emphasis on cooperation and more government intervention and hence limitations on trade openness and free competition. These types of regionalized economics can produce remarkable results for the well-being of the people in the countries in question. They have in fact produced spectacular results in development and growth through active international investment and trade for Japan as well as the miracle economies of Asia in the past three decades or so. Whether these economies can grow and develop strongly in the context of economic and financial globalization are the issues and problems discussed elsewhere in this book.

Part II

6
Japan and Prospects for Asia and World Economies

Tran Van Hoa

1. Introduction

Japan, a major industrialized economy in the world in modern times, is a complex society with a long history and a native religion (Shinto), consisting of nationalistic and aesthetic reverence to familiar places and traditions going back to the original Yamato dynasty which united the four main islands of the country in about 200 BC. Geographically the country lies far in East Asia and between the Pacific Ocean and the often treacherous Sea of Japan, not on the popular sea-routes linking Europe, the Middle East, the Subcontinent and Asia. Because of this position, Japan has for centuries been isolated from the world and sometimes it has successfully resisted the advances from the conquering forces of mainland Asia (for example, the two Mongolian expeditions of the thirteenth century). Since opening its door to the world after the Perry incident in 1871, Japan first saw the end of the Hoken Seido feudal system and since then it has successfully developed as a nation by mixing its traditional attitudes with western communications and ideas.

Since the reconstruction of its economy and constitution after the destruction of the World War II, Japan has in the past fifty years developed itself into a world economic power with widespread influences on the world's political and economic affairs. The development has been achieved with the help of the international community, starting with the Macarthur plan for Japan's reconstruction in the mid-1940s and an almost free trade environment for Japan's exports to the rest of the world's markets since. Being essentially a natural resource-poor country in Asia (the other Asian countries in a similar situation are: Singapore, Hong Kong and Taiwan), Japan's economic progress since this period has of necessity depended mainly on foreign investment initially, technology transfers from more economically advanced countries in Europe and North America, the improving quality of its labour force and production techniques, appropriate government fiscal and monetary policy, and last but not the least important, international trade (exports and imports).

Currently Japan was ranked third (after Singapore and the US) in terms of the criterion of income or GDP per head of the population after adjusting for the costs of living, had a budget larger than the combined budget of all Asian countries, and a relatively huge official development assistance (ODA) programme. In this context, Japan is well placed to play an important role in the economies of these Asian economies and, through them or through the linkage in international economic relations and transactions, in the economies of Europe, North and Latin Americas, the Middle East and Africa. This role is particularly important in the present Asian financial crisis in which major advanced countries, for mutually inclusive benefits, have actively sought ways to help or to rescue the economies in trouble and in which an additional economic turmoil occurring in Japan may eventually lead to a world-wide crisis leading to what is akin to the Great Depression of the 1930s.

This chapter first surveys the issues involved in the role of Japan in the world economy and its current economic problems and, secondly, analyses the methods or policies Japan can adopt or use to fix its economy's woes and to improve its international economic relations. Some assessment of the prospects of the world economy, which is closely related to what happens or will happen in Japan, will also be briefly discussed.

2.   Japan's economy and its role in the world

In 1960 Japan had a PPP (purchasing power parity) income per head of the population of $3 935.3 (see Figure 6.1) which was less than a quarter of that of the US and Switzerland, less than half of that of Sweden, Germany, the UK and Australia, but 13.2 per cent higher than that of Singapore ($3477.4). In 1997, at $20 290.4, this type of income in Japan was almost the same as that of Switzerland and higher than that of those other European countries and Australia. In fact, in 1997, it was exceeded only by the PPP income per head of Singapore ($29 201.5) and the US ($24 488.9).

In terms of the more conventional measure 'income per head at constant prices' however (see Figure 6.2), Japan in 1960 with an income of $5 101.0 was ranked below all the European countries listed but above Singapore ($2 504.2). In 1997 and with a constant price income of $26 300.5, it was ranked below Switzerland ($31 172.6) and Sweden ($27 263.9) but higher than the US ($24 488.9), Germany ($22 608.4), the UK ($18 914.9), Australia ($20 069.7) and Singapore ($21 029.1).

In 1967, Japan's exports to the world were $10 117.4 million as compared to its imports from it of $10 226.4 million (see Figure 6.3 and 6.4), incurring a trade deficit of $109.1 million or 1.08 per cent of its exports. It is of interest to note that during the 1967–96 period, 1967 (the first Egypt–Israel War) and 1974 (the first world oil crisis) were the only years in which Japan incurred a trade deficit, and 1973–75 and 1979–80 were the only periods in which Japan's trade surplus with the world was less than 5 per cent. This trade surplus was largest in 1986 at $100 891.4 million

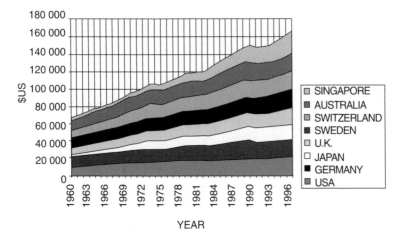

Figure 6.1   PPP income per head of selected countries

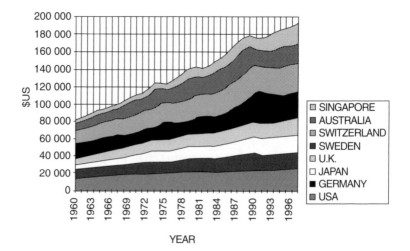

Figure 6.2   Constant price income per head in selected countries

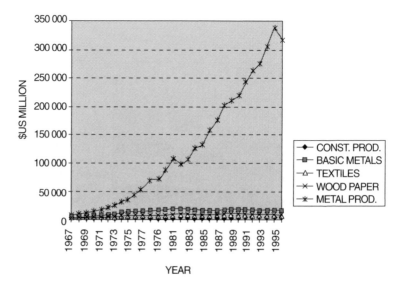

Figure 6.3a   Japan's major exports to the world

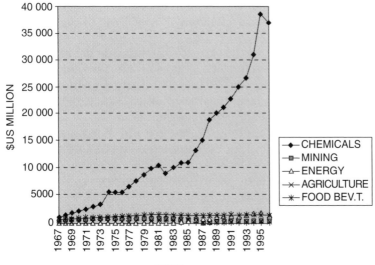

Figure 6.3b   Japan's major exports to the world

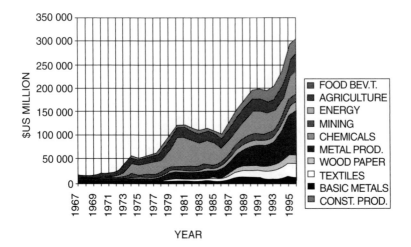

Figure 6.4   Japan's imports from the world

($209 096.4 million for exports and $108 204.9 million for imports) or 48.25 per cent of trade, followed in 1988 by $132 626.1 million or 42.1 per cent.

Since 1993, Japan's trade balance with the world has been declining with 39.7 per cent in 1993, 37.1 per cent in 1994, 30.9 per cent in 1995 and 21.8 per cent in 1996. While the growth of imports from the world to Japan has been positive since 1992, Japan's exports have been falling, especially since 1995.

The main sector of exports from the world to Japan since 1967 has been energy, but since 1993 this has been taken over by metal products (see Figure 6.5 (a) and 6.5 (b) for the patterns of change for the 23 components of the metal product export sector). The value of imported metal products to Japan in 1996 was $94 096.6 million and that of imported energy was $55 726.8. These values have a share in total imports of 30.1 per cent and 17.8 per cent respectively.

Textiles have also been growing steadily, but since 1989 they have been taken over by food, beverages and tobacco which now rank third in imports ($36 164.0 million or 11.6 per cent). Since 1967, the principal exports from Japan to the world were metal products

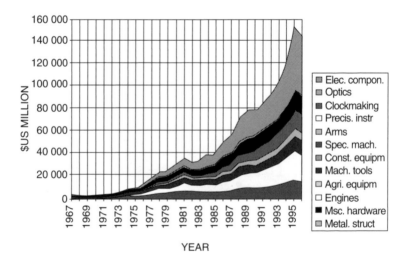

Figure 6.5a   Japan's metal product exports to the world

which in 1996 stood at $311 532.2 million, followed by chemicals at $37 642.8 million, by base metals at $18 931.1 million and by wood and paper products at $13 741.7 million.

It should be noted that Japan's relative share of world trade or exports is not the largest (see Figure 6.6). In 1967, this share for Japan was only 4.9 per cent of total trade which is the same as the share for the Arab world but below that of the Latin Americas (6.2 per cent), the US (16.4 per cent) and the European Union (39.4 per cent). In 1996, at 8.2 per cent, Japan's share ranked third after the European Union (41.0 per cent) and the US (11.6 per cent). Japan's gain in the share of world trade during 1967 to 1996 had therefore been achieved at the expense of the US, the Latin Americas, the Arab world and other countries such as the former USSR whose trade share had declined from 3.8 per cent in 1967 to 1.8 per cent in 1996. China's trade had made a significant growth from 0.7 per cent in 1967 to 3.3 per cent in 1996.

The above analysis of recent economic and export and import data (CHELEM, 1998) seems to indicate the relative importance of Japan as a leading economy (in terms of its GDP per head) in the world, its important role (ranked third) in international trade, its

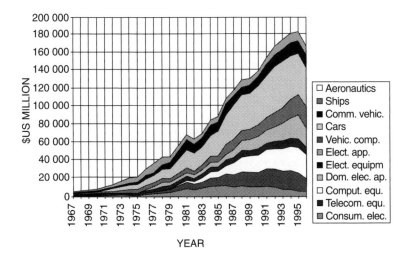

Figure 6.5b   Japan's metal product exports to the world

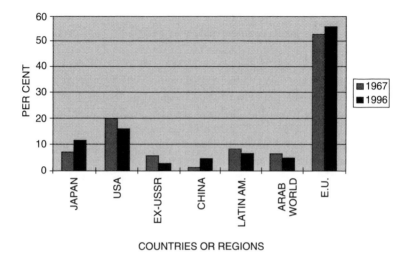

Figure 6.6   Shares of world trade for major countries and regions in 1967 and 1996

status as a major surplus trading country and the part metal products play in its economy's export activities. It also indicates the close link between Japan's domestic economic activities, international trade, balance of payments and foreign direct investment. All these lead subsequently to other activities with a social or political impact internationally. One of these activities is the official development assistance (ODA) programme for emerging, transitional and developing countries to help them with their economic development and modernization process.

Ironically, these characteristics of the Japanese economy also indicate its fragility: a slow-down in international trade and its exports may seriously affect the Japanese economy, and the contagion a Japan in crisis can produce world wide may be severe and damaging. One of the scenarios currently under intensive study by economists and financial analysts is: can an economic or financial crisis happening in Japan have a strong base to spread quickly and damagingly to the other countries that Japan is trading or dealing with. Conversely, the current Asian economic crisis cannot be overcome and its contagion cannot be arrested unless the Japanese economy is stable and strong with a positive growth in international trade and in domestic economic activities.

3. Japan's current economic and financial situation

While we noted earlier that Japan's exports have started declining significantly since 1995, this would indicate, because of the characteristics in the significance of international trade in the Japanese economy, that it has been in deep trouble since then. But it has taken a major Asian crisis with its serious contagion two years later, and such a major crisis as the collapse of the Long Term Credit Bank of Japan in September 1998, to convince the world, and especially Japanese authorities, that Japan should look at its own problems; they should consider how to fix them quickly for the sake of the international community's growth, development, trade, political stability and other welfare issues.

What are Japan's current problems? As we know them through commissioned government reports, mass media surveys and expert comments, Japan's problems cover a wide spectrum of issues, involve a magnitude of funds, and reflect more the way Japan has structured its society and has been conducting its economic, financial, industrial and social policies. These issues include in particular: a large number of bad loans made by Japan's banks and financial institutions in the past few years, a government that vacillates between paralysis and denial of national wrong-doings, a highly regulated society where the government and not the private sector still plays a big role in running the economy, the not-so-rosy long-term prospects for an aging population, and a racially homogeneous and male-dominated society (see Moschella, 1998).

More specifically, in recent years, Japan has to face the unthinkable spectre of a recession after many decades of spectacular, high and uninterrupted growth and trade expansion. Its stock market has to face the grim prospects of unpleasantly reduced earnings and a fall in its cross shareholding; its unemployment and bankruptcies are at record highs, and its people's spending and savings and its aggregate demand are severely restricted by a lack of tax reforms. In addition, as a result of unwise management and insufficient prudential control and supervision, Japan's banks, including some of the biggest names in the country, have collapsed one after another in a matter of weeks after posting a collective bad debt of about one trillion US dollars. These bad loans had resulted from the banks' excessive lending of the 1980s. As recently as the end of October in 1998, the Japanese jobless outlook had not improved after the long-awaited government kick-start programme was announced but, on the contrary, it had worsened (Japan Economy, *Internet*, November 1998). It is at this time that the government of Japan also received requests of 4 trillion yen to support a stimulus plan to rescue the economy from sliding further towards a depression. The current policy of keeping the yen high and the outlook of economic gloom have hurt the important part of Japan's exports and particularly its high-quality electronic firms (e.g., Matsushita Electric Industrial Co. and Sony) which, we saw earlier, have had a major role in the country's exports. Other Japanese companies, such as Mitsubishi Oil and Nippon Oil, and some big steelmakers, have all been feeling the pressure on their earnings.

All these issues have been seen by many experts in Japan and foreign economies as not crucial. This view was based on the strength of Japan's economy in the past decades, its sheer size in GDP and domestic savings (at $US 8.6 trillion), its international reserves and its monumental investment overseas. Things have changed however, and now even Japan's officials have to warn that even the US economy (the world's biggest debtor nation with falling saving rates) is vulnerable to the crisis in Japan. It is worse than that: a recent G7 announcement on a $90 billion measure to arrest world crises, while boosting New York and some Latin American markets (e.g. Brazil) late in October 1998, will have, according to many highly respected and influential government analysts, little impact on Japan's or Asia's problems. In addition, a $US 517 million bailout in public funds by the government of Japan may not be sufficient to help troubled banks with bad debts, which to date total one trillion US dollars. The downsizing by many Japanese companies (e.g. Daiwa Bank) of their overseas operations to cut costs in order to survive has also aggravated the damaging effect of Japan's crisis on other economies.

As Japanese economists and authorities have often claimed, the problems of Japan are specific to Japan or to the Japanese-style system and, as such, they are different from the woes of other countries in Asia or beyond. But we have demonstrated above that in spite of these claims, the fundamental problems in economic developments are based on a democratic and free-market system of a developing country, be it Japan or Malaysia, and that Japan's economic management, financial market, and banking institutions are not much different from those of other countries in crisis in Asia and beyond. Some examples here may be appropriate. Thailand was known to have unwisely invested domestic and foreign capital in improperly selected sectors, especially the real estate sector, and this has chiefly contributed to its economic crisis. Japan's banks have also made many reckless loans without providing adequate prudential safeguards and have created what is known as the 'debt legacy' of the country. Some major causes of Korea's crisis have been attributed to the excesses of the chaebols (big businesses) and bad government policy based on favouritism and bias. Japan's policy of strict government regulations and controls goes against the free-market environment of a modern economy. Some of the problems in Indonesia have been blamed on bad governance and corruption. But many cases of corporate and government corruption have also been exposed in Japan in recent years.

To some analysts, Japan's financial, social and political systems have many drawbacks and while they were good for the Japanese in Japan they were never the envy of the world. It was the Japanese companies that inspired awe: Toyota, Sony, NEC, Fujitsu, Toshiba, Mitsubishi, NTT, Matsushita, the Bank of Japan and so on. It is the decline of so many of those titans that is at the heart of the crisis issues. The extent of the decline is still unfolding and therefore difficult to estimate accurately. With the Nikkei stock average is still less than half of what it was a decade ago, it is easy to see, however, that the late 1980s was a foolish speculative bubble period in Japan. Where most individual and corporate investors in Japan went wrong was that they were wrong about the prospects for Japanese corporations. In the late 1980s it was in the information technology sector that, wisdom indicates, investment should have been made. Due to their lack of foresight and wisdom, Japanese companies had overlooked the computer, communications and semiconductor businesses during this period, and let such US companies as Microsoft, Intel, Cisco, Compaq and so many others capture the sector and create the wealth that has never been seen before in corporate history (Moschella, 1998).

The lack of competitiveness, which is due to the way things were done to a significant extent under government control or cooperation in Japan, extends far beyond the technology sector and on to such sectors as finance, banking, insurance, retail, telecommunications and services. While Japan's manufacturing companies are its most efficient firms, as they have been exposed to global competition and modern management practices, the non-manufacturing sectors above have been isolated from world-class rivals, allowing legendary levels of bureaucracy, overstaffing and other inefficiencies. While Citibank and Merrill Lynch can provide superior returns for investments from long-suffering Japanese savers, Japanese finance companies are quite happy with their long-standing lack of competitiveness. Japanese insurance and pension funds have not kept up with world standards, and online travel services reveal the absurdity of many Japanese airline and travel prices (Moschella, 1998).

While these problems have been diagnosed as the informal, qualitative or non-empirical causes of Japan's economic crisis, their impact on not only Japan but other world economies trading or dealing with it appear, nevertheless, serious and far-reaching. What are the prospects then for Japan's and other economies in Asia where the turmoil started and for the rest of the world, which has been watching political events and economic and financial developments in Japan with keen self-interest?

4. Japan's recovery plan and measures

With the advent of two major developments: the crisis in East Asia with its deep contagion and then the turmoil in Japan with its perceived worldwide damages, the world was taken almost by surprise. As the crises unfold almost unendingly, a number of national and international measures have been proposed and adopted for their recovery back to continued growth and sustainable development. The international measures have been introduced by the G7 and the Asia Pacific Economic Cooperation (APEC) forum and other similarly constructed bodies during their numerous meetings in recent months. The national measures in Japan were proposed by such august organizations as the Social and Economic Outlook Committee (SEOC) and the Economic Entity Role Committee (EERC).

In the case of the latter body, a report was submitted to the Economic Council after the deliberation of 13 meetings of the SEOC, 11 meetings of the EERC, and 93 meetings of 11 working groups between July 1997 and June 1998. This report outlines the measures Japan has to take to recover its economy and, by doing so, it will minimize the contagion's damage to the rest of the world's economies. Some of these measure have also been proposed in the set of comprehensive economic measures translated and circulated by the Economic Planning Agency of Japan in April 1998. The measures proposed to the Economic Council include:

- A scenario for recovery to growth path and sharing a proper sense of crisis: 'debt legacy' disposal, supply side structural reforms, aggregate demand stimulation, venture industries regarded as leading the overall economy, clear future outlook for macroeconomy and Japanese-style systems, labour market adjustments through deregulation.
- Macroeconomic outlook after structural reforms: a clear and fair market system, a society in harmony with the environment, and positive assets to future generations.
- The shape of the new social and economic system (the direction of reforms): Japanese-style market systems emphasizing cooperation over competition, Japan after its 'catch up growth' phase must pursue efficiency and the principle of competition, experiments to upgrade to a new system for future reforms, subsystem structural reforms must be advanced simultaneously.
- The actual shape of the new social and economic system: diverse employment system, diversifying corporate governance, privatizing the public sector, social security and medical system reforms, deregulation of education system, age-free and gender-free society, development of new core social economic entities in the new system.

5. Assessment of Japan's prospects

The above measures, as proposed by the various government agencies and committees, indicate the urgency and severity of the crisis in Japan in the face of the Asia currency turmoil and its contagion to the rest of the world economies. In formulating and proposing the measures it has been assumed that implementing them will get Japan to economic growth path and sustainable development, provide support to the role of the central government in social capital formation, prepare Japan well for the twenty-first century through structural reforms, improve social infrastructure and security, and provide funding support for Asia.

These measures are, to us, brave efforts on the part of the government of Japan and its agencies to kick-start the economy, to arrest the Asian contagion and to help, with the collaboration of the major economies in the world, prevent what is appearing to be another great world depression. But are these measures adequate, suitable or effective in the current climate of turmoil and crisis?

To us these measures will not be sufficient to avert the problems despite all the international efforts taken. A strong economy with a positive growth for Japan may not be able to prevent a deterioration in the balance of payments, if its people continue to live beyond their means. A fiscal policy to promote growth will fail to do so if government expenditure is focused on building roads and harbours and not on the financial and social infrastructure which Japan currently and desperately needs. A plan by Japan to improve its balance of trade may not be successful if such a major economy as China introduces a policy to gain a bigger share of world trade through subsidies or currency devaluation. Japan's experts have often talked about a Japanese-style free-market system, but Japan is, to outsiders, still a highly regulated society in which the government and its statutory authorities play a major and decisive part in running almost anything.

Japan's proposed measures still emphasize cooperation over competition as a driving force to achieve economic recovery and growth. In this environment, it is not surprising that a competitive spirit seems lacking in many other industries and government departments. The exception is the manufacturing industry which has had international exposure and interaction. A climate for such an important sector as the venture industries has not been strongly supported in Japan.

An important point that many commentators and analysts have overlooked in their debates on Japan's financial crisis and rescue policies is that Japan, as we have described above, is a resource-poor economy and its growth depends crucially on its international trade. While Japan has succeeded in almost perfecting its production-engineering techniques to produce goods which are better and cheaper than its trading rivals, its trade revenue and, therefore, its economy still depend on innovative and very high technology transfers from other advanced countries of the world to be highly competitive in trade, in finance, in human resource development, in the services sector, and in economic management in an economic globalization context.

Until such measures are formulated, introduced and implemented, the prospects for Japan's problems are not that good either for itself or for the world economies. The fact that no consensus by the world's major economies to use expansionary fiscal policy to arrest the crisis and promote growth has yet been agreed upon does not seem to augur well either. The crisis in Asia and its contagion may, on the other hand, demonstrate to the world that economic globalization is beneficial in both theory and practice only if the economies of the world cooperate. There is ample historical evidence in the past seventy years to indicate that this requirement in international economic relations is true now and for the future.

References

CHELEM Database, Paris: CEPII and WEFA, France, 1998.

Economic Council (1998), *Overview of the Joint Report of the Social and Economic Outlook Committee and the Economic Entity Role Committee*, June.

Economic Planning Agency (1998), *Summary of Comprehensive Economic Measures*, April.

Internet (1998), *Japan Economy*, November.

Morse, A. (1998), *Nikkei Seen Pressured by Grim Earnings, Internet*, November.

Moshella, D. (1998), 'Japan's Woes Expose Impossibility of Isolationism in the Internet Age', *Internet*, July.

7
Indonesia: The Road from Economic and Social Collapse

Charles Harvie

1. Introduction

Indonesia's economic performance over the past three decades has ranked among the best in the developing world, with real GDP growth averaging about 7 per cent annually since 1970. During this period the economy has become more diversified as an export-oriented manufacturing base has developed, reducing the country's dependency on the oil sector, and a dynamic private sector has evolved in conjunction with substantial inflows of foreign direct investment. A consistent adherence to prudent macroeconomic policies, the maintenance of high domestic investment and savings rates, and a market-oriented trade and exchange-rate regime provided the key to this success. Macroeconomic balance was maintained: the budget was balanced; inflation was kept at relatively low levels; current account deficits were moderate; and international reserves remained at comfortable levels. In addition, broad-based labour-intensive growth, together with sustained improvements in basic education and health services, dramatically reduced the incidence of poverty from 58 per cent in 1972 to 11 per cent, approximately 28 million people, by 1997, reflecting a strong commitment by the government to poverty reduction.

Despite its good macroeconomic fundamentals, Indonesia faced an abrupt shift in market sentiment from the middle of 1997, as the currency contagion, starting with Thailand, spread across the region. A major crisis of confidence afflicted the country which was reflected in a dramatic fall in the value of the rupiah and in equity prices, which became the largest in the region. From mid 1997 to mid 1998 the depreciation of the rupiah reached over 80 per cent, and the Jakarta stock exchange index fell by 50 per cent. These developments occurred despite strong corrective action by the government from the outset.

A steady deterioration in the economic environment occurred throughout the remainder of 1997, but by early 1998 the country experienced a further dramatic reversal in fortune leaving it in a very weak position. Annual per capita income fell from around $US 1,200 to $US 300; stock market capitalization was down from $US 118 billion to $US 17 billion; only 22 of Indonesia's 286 publicly listed companies were considered to be solvent; and only four firms remained with a market capitalisation of $US 500 million or more out of 49 from before the crisis. These adverse developments were further compounded by the social and economic upheavals in May 1998[1] which left the country on the edge of economic and political collapse. The distribution system was badly damaged, economic activity, including exports, generally disrupted, and business confidence severely shaken. As a result the exchange rate further substantially weakened rather than strengthening as envisaged in the April economic programme agreed between the IMF and the Indonesian government, and inflation began to increase at a rate higher than projected due to the collapse of the currency as well as the country's ongoing drought. Because of shortfalls in budgetary resources expenditures were reduced to unsustainable levels, with adverse consequences for social services and economic activity. In addition, large-scale liquidity support had to be provided to meet runs on a major private bank, Bank Central Asia, which was subsequently placed under the control of the bank restructuring agency (IBRA).

The new government under President Habibie, recognizing the severity of the crisis, committed itself to the rapid stabilization of the economy and to far-reaching structural reform. Changes to the macroeconomic framework as well as strengthening the social safety net, to cushion the escalating effects of the crisis on the poor, were seen as priorities. The most urgent priority, however, became the need to repair the distribution system and ensure adequate supplies of food and other necessities to all parts of the country in the face of a rapid deterioration in economic and social conditions. The need to move quickly to restructure the banking system comprehensively was also seen as a priority. Given the enormity of the tasks facing the government and the fragility of the economy, achieving these objectives will, until the economy recovers, require considerable additional financial support from the international community.

The remainder of this chapter proceeds as follows. Section 2 outlines the macroeconomic background in the build-up to the financial crisis. Section 3 focuses upon macroeconomic developments and the policy framework during 1998, while section 4 identifies the short- to medium-term economic and social prospects for the country. Finally, section 5 presents a summary of the major conclusions from this chapter.

2.   Macroeconomic background

Indonesia became afflicted by the Asian currency contagion in July 1997, and subsequently experienced sizeable declines in both its exchange rate and stock markets. This reversal in the country's economic outlook followed two years in which it had been amongst the best performing economies in South East Asia, and it appeared, at least initially, to be in much better shape to weather such a storm. There was general agreement in the middle of 1997 by economists in foreign banks, the IMF and World Bank that its economy was fundamentally sound and not at risk of suffering Thailand's problems. The country was experiencing smaller current account deficits and allowed its exchange rate to float within a wider band. It did, however, share problems of an emerging oversupply in the property market, a relatively weak banking system and endemic institutional corruption.

Tables 7.1 and 7.2 indicate why, before the onset of the crisis, its performance was generally regarded as being satisfactory. The country had experienced strong growth during the five years prior to the currency contagion, achieving a GDP growth rate of 8 per cent in 1996 which was only slightly less than that achieved in 1995. Early growth predictions in 1997 were for growth to be at round the same rate for 1997, however, the economic turmoil after July 1997 resulted in a GDP growth rate of only 4.5 per cent. By the end of 1997 and into early 1998 Indonesia began to experience a dramatic reversal of economic fortune, which intensified throughout 1998.

Prior to the financial turmoil, growth in demand came primarily from domestic sources. Private investment was a key driving force with capital expenditure increasing by 12.2 per cent in 1996. Private consumption, which accounted for 58.5 per cent of GDP, increased by 9.2 per cent in 1996. On the production side the major sources of growth were derived from non oil/gas manufacturing output, accounting for 22 per cent of GDP in 1996, which expanded annually by between 9.3 and 12.5 per cent over the period 1992–97 and, even more significantly, the construction sector which expanded annually over the same period by between 10.8 and 14.9 per cent. Of increasing significance was the services sector which experienced annual growth of between 7.1 and 8.3 per cent during 1992–97, while agricultural output growth was considerably less and more volatile falling to 1.9 per cent in 1996 after a strong year in 1995. Such impressive and consistent growth outcomes contributed to a noticeable increase in GDP per capita from $US 690 in 1992 to $US 1,147 in 1996 but declining to $US 1,066 in 1997. A key component underlying this was high domestic saving which contributed to a correspondingly high level of domestic investment (see Table 7.1). However, the gap between saving and investment has been increasing and is reflected in a steady deterioration in the current account deficit.

Indonesia experienced relatively high nominal interest rates during the period of the 1990s. More recently, after 1993, high interest rates were engineered by Bank Indonesia to conduct a tight monetary policy with the objective of constraining the growth of consumer credit and thereby: reduce excess demand within the economy; reduce inflationary pressure; and keep the current account deficit at manageable levels. It also enabled the country to increase its trade surpluses and to expand its foreign exchange reserves. However, the maintenance of high domestic interest rates also contributed to the build up of foreign borrowing, particularly by the corporate sector, as a means of circumventing the high domestic costs of funding. The financial crisis in the second half of 1997 produced a sharp increase in the interest rate as the authorities tried to stem the downward slide of the rupiah. A sharp rise in interest rates formed a key component of the conditions for the IMF rescue package granted to Indonesia after October 1997, but had severe implications for the highly leveraged corporate sector.

Table 7.1 Indonesia's recent macroeconomic performance 1992–97

	1992	1993	1994	1995	1996	1997
GDP Growth Rate (%)	7.2	7.3	7.5	8.2	8.0	4.5
GDP Nominal ($US bn)	128.5	158.5	174.0	192.2	227.4	214.6
GDP Per Capita ($US)	690	840	900	1023	1147	1066
Gross National Saving (% of GDP)	32.3	32.8	31.9	31.4	33.7	35.2
Gross Domestic Investment (% of GDP)	33.9	34.5	33.7	34.8	37.7	39.2
Real Growth in Sectoral Output (%):						
Agriculture	6.6	1.4	0.5	4.0	1.9	—
Construction	10.8	12.1	14.9	12.9	12.4	—
Manufacturing	9.7	9.3	12.5	11.1	11.0	—
Services	7.5	8.3	7.1	7.7	7.5	—
Interest Rate (%):						
Discount Rate, End of Period	13.50	8.82	12.44	13.98	12.8	20.0
CPI (%)	7.5	9.7	8.5	9.4	7.9	6.6

Sources: IMF, *World Economic Outlook*, Interim Assessment, December 1997
IMF, *International Financial Statistics*, January 1998
Ministry of Finance, Indonesia
Author's calculations

Table 7.2 Indonesia's trade, balance of payments and exchange rate (1992–98)

	1992/93	1993/94	1994/95	1995/96	1996/97*	1997/98**
Merchandise Exports (FOB) ($US Billion)	35.3	36.5	42.2	47.7	51.7	56.2
Merchandise Imports (FOB) ($US Billion)	30.3	33.3	37.9	41.5	46.6	50.7
Balance on Merchandise Trade ($US Billion)	5.0	3.2	4.3	6.2	5.1	5.4
Balance on Services Trade ($US Billion)	-10.5	-10.3	-11.5	-13.2	-13.9	-15.2
Current Account Balance ($US Billion)	-2.6	-3.0	-3.3	-6.9	-8.8	-9.8
Per cent of GDP	-1.8	-1.8	-1.8	-3.4	-4.0	-4.0
Merchandise Exports (FOB) (% Change on Previous Year)	18.8	3.4	15.6	13.4	9.7	8.7
Merchandise Imports (FOB) (% Change on Previous Year)	10.2	9.9	13.8	27.0	5.4	8.8
Gross External Debt	83.7	89.3	101.2	108.8	120.2	137.4#
Debt Service Ratio	32.2	33.4	33.7	34.8	33.7	—

Table 7.2 Continued

	1992/93	1993/94	1994/95	1995/96	1996/97*	1997/98**
Foreign Exchange Reserves***	10.5	11.3	12.1	13.7	18.3	16.6
Exchange Rate*** ($US- Rupiah)	2029.9	2087.1	2160.8	2248.6	2342.3	2909.4

Sources: IMF, *International Financial Statistics*, January 1998
Ministry of Finance, Indonesi
Department of Foreign Affairs and Trade, Australia–Country
Economic Brief, Indonesia, August 1997.

Notes:

*   Preliminary figures

**   Budget

***   Calendar year figures

\#   End 1997

The country's inflation performance has also been impressive, as indicated in Table 7.1. The government's tight monetary policy proved to be successful, with inflation remaining well below 10 per cent. Year average consumer price inflation was 7.9 per cent in 1996, down from 9.4 per cent in 1995 and 6.6 per cent in 1997. Expectations were for a considerable increase in inflation during 1998 with the elimination of subsidies by the government on items such as fuel and food as part of a renegotiated IMF rescue package in the first quarter as well as that increase due to the weakness of the currency and the on-going drought. Predictions of an inflation rate of 80 per cent for 1998 have been advanced (see below).

From Table 7.2 it can be observed that Indonesia's merchandise exports totalled $US 51.7 billion in 1996–97, up by 9.7 per cent from 1995–96. This was a relatively weak performance compared with Indonesia's export growth of 13.4 per cent in the previous period 1995–96, and came despite stronger world oil prices. Manufactured export growth was only around 8 per cent, the slowest recorded in the previous 5 years. While the performance in 1996 was weaker than that in 1995, overall this was a relatively good performance in light of the regional export downturn, with exports of higher technology products performing quite well. Labour intensive exports, however, did not perform particularly well. Merchandise exports were budgeted to expand to $US 56.2 billion for 1997–98 representing a further 8.7 per cent growth, but the rapidly deteriorating economic situation in East Asia made this look overly optimistic. Indonesia's non-oil/gas exports have been a driving force behind economic growth, averaging an annual rate increase of 20 per cent between 1985 and 1995. However, non-oil/gas export growth reached just 9 per cent in 1996. This slowdown was not unique to Indonesia but was common throughout most of East Asia. Indeed, Indonesia was less affected than most of the other economies in the region. Manufactured goods growth remained at the heart of the government's economic priorities, and industrial exports grew to comprise 64.5 per cent of all exports and over 84 per cent of Indonesia's non-oil/gas exports. The relative importance of oil and gas exports has been declining steadily since the early 1980s. In 1996, however, strong prices as a result of the US/Iraq crisis mid year, saw oil and gas exports grow at over 12 per cent. But the trend towards decline in oil and gas export dependence should continue.

Merchandise import growth declined dramatically from 27 per cent in 1995 to 5.4 per cent in 1996, and amounted to $US 46.6 billion. In 1996 machinery and equipment accounted for 40 per cent of all imports, with industrial products accounting for another 32 per cent. A large proportion of the import growth in 1996 was therefore attributable to capital equipment and intermediate goods, which are closely associated with the expansion of foreign direct investment. It was budgeted that import growth would pick up again during 1997–98 to 8.8 per cent, but in the light of the financial crisis this has not materialized.

Unlike many other countries in the region, Indonesia is in the advantageous position of running consistent and sizeable merchandise trade surpluses due substantially to the export of oil and gas, which have contributed considerably to the country's accumulation of foreign exchange reserves. This surplus peaked during 1995–96 at $US 6.2 billion. During 1996–97 Indonesia maintained a sizeable surplus due to the large slowdown in import growth, as well as from weaknesses in the Japanese yen and higher global oil prices. As a consequence the relatively poor performance by Indonesia's non-oil exports in 1996 was masked.

However, a lingering weakness for the country relates to the services trade deficit, which has continued its trend increase continuously during the period of the 1990s. In 1992–93 it stood at $US 10.5 billion rising to $US 13.9 billion in 1996–97. This large and growing deficit is primarily due to: the country's dependence on foreign shipping for both international and domestic trade; the large proportion of foreign professionals employed in Indonesian businesses; and, most significantly, the cost of its foreign debt (interest payments which are recorded as service imports in Indonesia's balance of payments statistics). A sustained appreciation of the yen, in particular, or depreciation of the rupiah increases Indonesia's debt-serving costs,[2] and has a severe impact on the services deficit.

As a consequence, primarily of developments in the services deficit, Indonesia's current account deficit has been steadily deteriorating in recent years. It increased from $US 2.6 billion (1.8 per cent of GDP) in 1992–93 to $US 8.8 billion (4 per cent of GDP) in 1996–97. However, this was considered manageable by the authorities. Indeed, Indonesia's current account balance in 1996, as a per cent of GDP, compared very favourably with that of its regional neighbours (see Harvie, 1999).

Strong capital inflows, particularly during the latter part of 1996 and the early part of 1997 in response to high interest-rate differentials, were more than sufficient to finance the growing current account deficit in 1996–97. This enabled Indonesia to achieve an overall balance-of-payments surplus and led to a sharp increase in foreign exchange reserves held by the central bank. Foreign direct investment has played an important role in attracting such foreign capital inflows, and this was encouraged following the liberalization of investment laws in 1994. According to Indonesia's balance of payments statistics, realized foreign direct investment inflows to Indonesia amounted to some $US 6.5 billion in 1996, up from $US 2 billion in 1994. The five largest foreign investors to date have been Japan, UK, Singapore, Hong Kong and the USA. In 1996, Japanese investment accounted for over 25 per cent of Indonesia's foreign direct investment approvals for that calendar year, and around 15 per cent of the projects. Current investment approvals in Indonesia reached $US 29.9 billion in 1996, down slightly on 1995 record levels. However, since 1994, like many other countries in East Asia, the country increasingly relied upon portfolio or equity capital flows to offset its current account deficits. The rapid withdrawal of such short-term funds in 1997 played a crucial role in the currency crisis.

Indonesia's foreign debt is estimated to have reached $US 137.4 billion at the end of 1997. This debt is divided approximately evenly between government and private sector borrowers, but more recently it came to light that the private sector had accumulated some $US 74 billion in foreign debt. Hence most of the debt, approximately 54 per cent, is now private debt. Government debt payments declined during 1996 as a result of a depreciation of the yen and earlier efforts to repay debts ahead of schedule, but the sharp depreciation of the rupiah had an adverse impact on government debt-servicing costs in 1997. In 1996 the government became increasingly concerned about the growing level of private sector debt, and began monitoring closely private sector foreign borrowing and restricting government guarantees and borrowing by government-owned companies. These concerns understated the problems of Indonesian companies exposed to US dollar liabilities following a drop in the exchange rate of the rupiah. While foreign debt is high, and represents a constraint on the flexibility of development policy in Indonesia, the country has had an excellent record in servicing its debts since the 1970s. International lenders, including the World Bank, also considered that borrowed funds were generally put to good use in supporting investment rather than recurrent expenditure.

Official reserves rose to $US 18.3 billion (around 5 months of merchandise exports) at the end of 1996–97, but fell to $US 16.6 billion at the end of 1997 due to the onset of the financial turmoil. By the first quarter of 1998 foreign reserves were estimated still to be around $US 17 billion.

The exchange rate experienced a continual depreciation relative to the US dollar during the period of the 1990s. This was the deliberate policy of the authorities, where a traditional targeted depreciation annually of between 4 and 5 per cent existed. However, during 1996 the exchange rate and stock market were major beneficiaries of foreign investment, primarily portfolio, inflows. In February 1997 the Jakarta stock exchange was trading at an all time high, despite rioting that broke out across Java, and the rupiah had depreciated by just 3.2 per cent for the whole of 1996 which was well below the central bank's traditional target.

After December 1995 Bank Indonesia had widened its exchange-rate band from 2 to 8 per cent, enabling more leeway in managing the economy. This put the country in a relatively advantageous position in comparison to the more rigid exchange-rate regimes operated by some of its neighbours. However, the collapse of the Thai baht after it was floated on 2 July 1997 immediately raised doubts about the viability of exchange rate-arrangements in neighbouring countries, including that of Indonesia. The strongest initial pressures emerged in the Philippines and the spill-over effects then spread to Malaysia where the authorities opted to allow the ringgit to depreciate rather than raise interest rates, and also to Indonesia where on 21 July the rupiah fell sharply within the official intervention band. In a pre-emptive move the authorities widened the intervention band from 8 to 12 percentage points immediately following the float of the Philippine peso. Subsequent measures to tighten liquidity conditions in Indonesia failed to stem the growing exchange market pressures, and the authorities allowed the rupiah to float on 14 August.

This brief review of Indonesia's macroeconomic performance before the onset of the financial crisis suggests that the economic fundamentals of the economy appeared to be relatively strong, and certainly not as bad as the situation in Thailand. Strong economic growth, relatively low inflation from an historical perspective arising from a tight monetary policy, low budget deficits, high domestic savings, growth of exports which despite the slowdown in 1996 compared well with its regional neighbours, a steady accumulation of foreign exchange reserves, a declining debt-service ratio, and a rising but still favourable and manageable current-account deficit. Of most concern was the increase in the resource gap between saving and investment, reflected in the rising current account deficit and increasing reliance on foreign savings to fund this. While FDI played an important role in this process there was an increasing reliance on foreign borrowing. Hence gross external debt was rising. About half of this in 1996–97 was owed by the private sector and denominated in hard currency including US dollars and, of particular significance, Japanese yen. This was of an increasingly short-run duration and considerably larger than the country's foreign exchange reserves. As a consequence the country had become increasingly vulnerable to adverse developments in the exchange rate, such as through a loss of confidence and developments in world interest rates, and this vulnerability further intensified during 1997.

3. Macroeconomic developments during 1998 and the policy framework

The economic situation in Indonesia deteriorated rapidly by the beginning of 1998. The major factors behind this included: the increasingly desperate need to restructure sizeable, unhedged, private foreign borrowing; the growing fragility of the financial system due to poor regulatory and legal foundations; an apparent reluctance by the government to implement policies agreed with the IMF as part of a financial rescue package; an ageing leader with no clear successor; spectacular wealth accumulation through 'KKN' (the Indonesian acronym for 'corruption, cronyism, and nepotism'); and increasing social unrest. However, few could have predicted the speed or the scale of the crisis affecting Indonesia during the period of the crisis since. This included: the collapse of the exchange rate from Rp 2500 to the US dollar at the beginning of the crisis to a low of Rp 15 000 to the $US, representing one of the largest real exchange rate depreciations in the post-World War II era; a turn-around in economic growth of 22 percentage points (from positive 7.8 per cent in 1996/97 to possibly negative 10–15 per cent for 1998/99) comparable only to that experienced by industrial economies during the Great Depression of the 1930s; the country experienced a $US 22 billion reversal of private capital flows, from inflows of $US 10 billion in 1996/97 to outflows of $US 12 billion in 1997/98, which was nearly as large as the total net private capital flows during the entire decade from 1985–95; the financial and economic crisis has been accompanied by natural disasters, including a drought which reduced rice harvests and agricultural production generally and severe localized droughts contributed to uncontrollable forest fire; the price of oil, Indonesia's key export commodity, fell to $US 13 a barrel, its lowest level in real terms in thirty years; enormous political developments were also taking place. This historic combination of events created severe economic and social dislocation in the country. While Indonesia is justly proud of its rapid poverty reduction since the 1970s, the present crisis will see large-scale reversals of that progress.

The continued rapid depreciation of the rupiah, in conjunction with the country's worst drought in fifty years, resulted in a large increase in prices. The financial position of the domestic banking system dramatically deteriorated, and Bank Indonesia granted large-scale liquidity support which contributed to additional pressure on the exchange rate and international reserves. In addition foreign banks cut trade and other credit lines to Indonesian banks, resulting in domestic enterprises having difficulty in obtaining the imported inputs needed for production. After a number of false starts (see Harvie, 1999), and against this background of rapid economic deterioration, the Indonesian government and the IMF reached agreement over a programme necessary for the recovery of the economy and for the advancement of further financial assistance. This was outlined in the Statement of Development Policy of 8 April 1998, the objective of the reform programme being to stabilize the economy and achieve a recovery while shielding the poor from the worst effects of the crisis.

Despite the agreed programme and the likelihood of expanded international financial assistance, the economic situation and outlook worsened after April 1998. The country was shaken by social unrest in May which resulted in the resignation of President Suharto and the appointment of President Habibie. The social disturbances during this period and their political ramifications had a serious effect on the economy,[3] resulting in further disruptions to economic activity and a damaging decline in business confidence. The country was close to both economic and social collapse, with expectations for a decline in GDP of between 10–15 per cent during 1998 and for inflation to increase to around 80 per cent being advanced by the authorities. The exchange rate depreciated by 50 per cent, from about Rp 8000 at the beginning of May 1998 to Rp 16 000 by mid June. In a thin market, the exchange rate was very volatile and dominated by sudden shifts in market confidence, and became particularly difficult to forecast. A conservative monetary policy kept interest rates near 60 per cent, imports fell by about 20 per cent in the first five months of 1998, and export growth also slowed. The macroeconomic framework remained subject to unusually large uncertainty. As a consequence of these adverse economic and social developments the agreed April programme was amended in June, although the basic framework remained.

The April programme provided the basis for the policy response to the economic difficulties facing the economy, and consisted of the following key components:

(a) maintaining macroeconomic stability with an emphasis on stabilizing the rupiah at a level more in line with the underlying strengths of the Indonesian economy, primarily through a tightening of monetary policy,

(b) reforming and strengthening the banking system,

(c) providing a framework for comprehensively addressing the debt problem of private corporations, emphasizing the need for its restructuring,

(d) strengthening the implementation of structural reforms to create the foundations for a more efficient and competitive economy, and improved governance,

(e) restoring trade financing to a normal basis, allowing domestic production and especially the export sector to recover.

The rapid deterioration of the economy after May 1998 focused increasingly upon another key component:

(f) implementing of measures to protect the poor, sustain key human resource investments, and to maintain food security and the distribution system.

Each of these components was seen as being necessary for restoring stability, regaining the confidence of international investors, and resuming growth. The government anticipated that the programme would be reinforced by financial support from the international community, including trade financing and the provision of food and medical aid. Each of these components is now discussed briefly in turn.

Macroeconomic management
Fiscal policy

A central feature of the April and June programmes was the limitation of the budget deficit to a level that could be offset by additional foreign financing. The pressures on the budget and fiscal management, however, intensified with the deepening of the crisis. The depreciation of the exchange rate, through its impact on the cost of subsidies and debt service, falling tax revenues, the further decline in oil prices, and the escalating costs of bank restructuring, resulted in a sharp increase in the fiscal deficit. In addition, given the severity of the crisis and its disproportionate impact on the poor, there was an urgent need to strengthen the social safety net to alleviate the impact of higher unemployment and underemployment and the greater incidence of poverty.

The decline of oil prices, together with the collapse of business activity, was expected to reduce government revenue from about 16.2 per cent of GDP in fiscal year 1997/98 to 14.1 per cent in fiscal year 1998/99. To increase overall revenue the government planned to raise about 1.6 per cent of GDP in capital revenues by divesting shares in twelve state companies, including Indosat and Telkom. This will push total revenues to 15.7 per cent of GDP. The overall budgetary cost of the social safety net programmes was estimated at about 7.5 per cent of GDP. Food, fuel, electricity, medicine and other subsidies are estimated, on the basis of current prices, to amount to about 6.2 per cent of GDP in 1998/99, about 4 percentage points higher than envisaged in April and up from 3.1 per cent in 1997/98. In addition, the government increased expenditures on: labour-intensive public works, targeted at poor and vulnerable regions and households; scholarships for poor primary and junior secondary school students; and medical supplies. The UN World Food Programme also established food for work programmes, concentrated in drought-affected areas. Budgetary allocations for health were increased, with emphasis on spending directed to the vulnerable groups, including village health centres and immunization programmes. Most of the needed savings to keep the budget deficit down as much as possible were expected to come from cuts in infrastructure projects. In collaboration with the Asian Development Bank and World Bank, cuts or delays to projects amounting to 2.5 per cent of GDP were envisaged.

The net effect is that the overall fiscal deficit is expected[4] to be about 8.5 per cent of GDP for fiscal year 1998/99, more than double the April estimate of 3.8 per cent. Little more than half of this could be financed from identified and committed external funds. The Indonesian government has been attempting to organize exceptional external financing to fill the remaining gap in close consultation with the IMF. A deficit of this magnitude, while justified by the severity of the present crisis, is not sustainable. The overall deficit in the 1999/2000 budget is envisaged to be smaller as a per cent of GDP, partly as a result of measures to raise revenue and reduce subsidies.

Monetary policy and the banking system

Tight monetary policy is regarded by the authorities as being essential if the exchange rate is to stabilize and inflation decline. This resulted in short-term interest rates rising to well over 50 per cent by mid 1998, resulting in a crippling effect upon the already stressed corporate sector. The need to reduce interest rates as quickly as possible should be seen as a major priority, but is unlikely in the immediate future. The monetary programme target was shifted towards that of net domestic assets (NDA) of Bank Indonesia instead of base money as agreed with the IMF in October 1997. This change was made, as it was seen as being essential to curb the expansion of bank credit which had grown rapidly. This required firm control of liquidity support to banks. Limits on NDA and net international reserves were used as performance criteria for the operation of monetary policy. The continued weakness of the rupiah and the danger of an inflationary spiral resulted in the authorities holding base money and NDA broadly constant during the latter half of 1998. Due to considerable uncertainty about developments in the economy, monetary policy was kept under continual review, and adjusted as necessary in light of developments in particular in the exchange rate and inflation.

To enhance the effectiveness of monetary management Bank Indonesia switched from a system in which interest rates on central bank paper (SBIs) were set administratively, to an auction system for these instruments. The changeover began with auctions of one-month paper in July 1998, with the objective of expanding this to a full range of maturities. Auctions of SBIs were to become the primary means for conducting open market operations by end September 1998. In addition to strengthening monetary control, this would enable a fully market-determined term structure of interest rates to emerge. With the perceived need to hold NDA and base-money constant, interest rates were likely to remain high in the near term but anticipated to decline as financial markets stabilized. Additionally, in order to provide Bank Indonesia with the autonomy for conducting monetary policy, the preparation of legislation on central bank independence was accelerated, and submitted to parliament at the end of September 1998.

Reforming and strengthening the banking system

The condition of banks deteriorated continuously during 1998, and the highest priority was to be given to the implementation of a comprehensive solution to the problems of the banking system, focusing upon weak banks and the establishment of a soundly functioning banking system. This is an essential precondition for the recovery of the corporate sector. A key element of the strategy involved measures to strengthen relatively sound bank, partly through the infusion of new capital. The approach to the weak banks involved moving swiftly to recapitalize, merge or effectively close them, while maintaining the commitment to guarantee all depositors and creditors. Decisions regarding individual banks were to be based on uniform and transparent criteria, drawing as appropriate from the results of portfolio reviews by international accounting firms. A high-level Financial Sector Advisory Committee was established to advise on the coordination of all the necessary actions for bank restructuring.

The banking system's financial trouble was compounded by the economic and social unrest after May 1998. One of its more immediate effects was the collapse of depositor confidence in the largest private bank in Indonesia – Bank Central Asia. The bank was placed under IBRA management on 29 May 1998. Many of the other national banks require urgent action to resolve their bad debts and to restructure their portfolios. The government was also concurrently acting to resolve the problems of weak and insolvent banks and to identify and revitalize some relatively well-managed banks, helping them restart lending to creditworthy customers and to reintegrate into interbank and international financial markets.

Bank Indonesia, with assistance from the Asian Development Bank, has been reviewing the portfolios of the three largest private banks, and several other private banks, with the objective of establishing their financial credentials and assisting them to regain access to trade facilities and interbank lines. The authorities are hoping that these banks can restart lending as soon as possible, and that they will eventually become the potential core around which an efficient and restructured banking system could be organized. To encourage them in this direction, Bank Indonesia and the Ministry of Finance are considering providing two-tier capital, generally in the form of subordinated loans, as well as entering into discussions with foreign banks for possible investments in Indonesia's banking sector. Indonesia's Bank Restructuring Agency (IBRA) has made progress in the task of restructuring troubled banks and resolving their stock of bad debts. Reviews of the first six banks (with combined assets totalling about 30 per cent of the total combined assets of the 54 banks) was completed in June 1998. Reviews of 47 more were completed by the end of July.

Of particular concern has been the scarcity of import and pre-shipment export finance, which could severely damage non-oil export earnings. This problem is being addressed through a variety of means. First, Bank Indonesia has established a cash collateral facility with ten foreign banks to ensure that country risk is not a barrier to the confirmation of loans and credits by correspondent foreign banks. Second, the Frankfurt debt accord included a trade finance component. Third, JEXIM extended a $US 1 billion loan to cover confirmation of import loans and credits opened on Indonesian banks and to provide working capital loans for imported inputs for export production. The World Bank has also provided technical assistance to Bank Indonesia to facilitate trade financing for developing schemes that will support renewed provision of pre-shipment trade finance by Indonesian Banks.

Corporate debt restructuring and bankruptcy legislation

The financial restructuring of the corporate sector is also crucial for economic recovery, and is essential for the establishment of a sound banking sector. Most corporate debt is relatively short-term, denominated in foreign currencies and typically unhedged. The depreciation of the rupiah and the compression of domestic demand during the period of the financial crisis has resulted in virtually all enterprises having difficulty in meeting their external and domestic debt-service obligations.

Extensive discussions in regard to such obligations have taken place between government representatives, the debtors' 'contact committee', and the creditors' 'steering committee', culminating in a debt agreement in Frankfurt on 4 June 1998. This agreement comprised three components: a framework for restructuring the foreign currency denominated debt of enterprises; a scheme to reschedule interbank debts; and an arrangement to maintain a minimum level of trade finance. Participation by debtors and creditors in this debt restructuring scheme was totally voluntary. Each debtor and creditor was expected to re-negotiate the debt, agree on possible debt reductions, debt/equity swaps, or other characteristics and the repayment stream within this framework. To participate in the scheme the terms of re-negotiated loans must have a minimum tenor of eight years, and a three-year grace period. The scheme will provide a framework through the Indonesian Debt Restructuring Agency (INDRA) for the voluntary restructuring of the debt of corporations to foreign banks on terms that are consistent with Indonesia's overall external payments capacity, and provide cashflow relief to domestic enterprises. It is envisaged that domestic as well as foreign creditors will participate in debt workouts for individual companies, with all creditors sharing in the burden of providing the necessary relief. In some cases debt writedowns will be needed. IBRA, especially its asset management unit, will be the major participant in many workouts.

While the Frankfurt agreement is important, it will not by itself solve the corporate sector's problems. An effective bankruptcy system is an essential part of the corporate debt restructuring strategy, without which debtors may be reluctant to negotiate with their creditors. Hence, the government is also continuing work to identify and remove obstacles to corporate restructuring within the legal and regulatory framework and to facilitate restructuring. A government regulation in lieu of law was issued in April 1998 to modernize the bankruptcy system and provide for the fair and expeditious resolution of commercial disputes. In this regard a special administrative court and procedures for bankruptcy became effective on 20 August, 120 days after the date of enactment of the regulation, which encouraged enterprises and creditors to the negotiating table, and facilitated the expeditious restructuring of failed companies.

Structural policies

The programme of structural reforms is aimed at enhancing the economy's transparency and governance, and making the policy framework more market friendly and environmentally friendly. It includes reforming trade policies, opening more sectors of the economy to competition, and privatization. All scheduled tariff reductions have been implemented and monopolies for cloves and plywood marketing have been dismantled. Forestry resource rents and export taxes on crude and refined palm oil have been introduced after a brief delay. Privatization is progressing on schedule, and seven additional enterprises to be partially privatized during 1998/99 have been identified – Bukit Asam, Jasa Marga, Pelabuhan Indonesia II, Pelabuhan Indonesia III, Angkasa Pura II, Perkebunan Nusatara IV and Krakatau Steel. Investment banks were appointed to make the necessary preparations for each of these enterprises, in addition to the five that are already privatized (Telkom, Indosat, Semen Gresik, Tambang Timah and Aneka Tambang). Part of the preparatory work needed is the formulation of a regulatory framework for privatized operations, to ensure that privatized state monopolies do not become private monopolies inconsistent with the proposed competition policy. Despite the depressed state of the economy, taking into account the interest that has been expressed by foreign investors, the government is confident that the projected receipts from privatization of $US 1.5 billion for the 1998/99 budget can be realized. The planned sales of shares in the domestic and international telecommunications corporations will provide a substantial part of this total.

The new government of President Habibie has also moved towards improving governance and transparency. A number of measures have been taken that go beyond the original programme. Central among these is a widespread effort to review government contracts that were offered through corruption, collusion and nepotism. International standard audits were due to be completed for Pertamina, PLN (the power company), BULOG and the Reforestation Fund by the end of 1998. Investment regulations have been changed to give the Minister for Investment final authority to approve all applications for investment up to $US 100 million. Previously, all applications over $US 100 000 required presidential approval. Finally, the government has ratified ILO Convention 87, ensuring the rights of association and assembly.

Restoring trade finance

The large decline in the country's trade credit, particularly since the crisis of May 1998, is of considerable concern since it jeopardizes exports. Part of the problem has been the unwillingness of foreign banks to confirm letters of credit, but this is being addressed through the assistance recently provided by JEXIM, export cover from a number of export credit agencies, and the Frankfurt trade facility agreement with foreign banks. A major remaining problem is the reluctance of domestic banks to open letters of credit except on a cash basis or to provide pre-shipment credit, because of the weak state of the corporate sector. As a temporary solution, Bank Indonesia established during July a pre-shipment export guarantee programme to facilitate import and pre-shipment export financing for exporters holding export letters of credit. The guarantee will be provided for a fee on a loan-by-loan basis, and will be partial so that risk is shared with the domestic bank. The programme was designed to be temporary and initially limited to about $US 0.5 billion. The risk associated with the guarantee would be borne by the government rather than Bank Indonesia, and was believed to be justified due to the severity of the economic crisis.

Efforts to protect the poor, maintain food security and the distribution system

The number of poor in Indonesia was likely to double during 1998, and as a consequence the need to protect this vulnerable group within the country from the worst effects of the crisis has become imperative. Focus has been placed upon ensuring adequate supplies of basic commodities, on maintaining effective distribution networks, on establishing labour-intensive employment programmes to ensure the poor continue to have adequate purchasing power, and the implementation of initiatives to maintain access to quality basic education and health. Strengthening these programmes has contributed most of the increase in the country's fiscal deficit, however, the government is strongly committed to protect the poor but additional external support to help fund this effort will be required.

The government has emphasized the need to ensure that there are adequate supplies of essential commodities, especially rice, and that these are available easily through the distribution system at affordable prices. BULOG, for example, has increased its import target for rice in 1998/99 from 2.85 million tons to 3.1 million tons. Special measures have been introduced to ensure that domestic markets have adequate supplies of cooking oil at reasonable prices. Food subsidies in general were increased substantially during 1998, contributing to the substantial increase in the fiscal deficit, as part of a broader effort to ensure food security for the poor. The subsidy on kerosene, the petroleum fuel which is most important to the poor, has increased sharply because its price has remained unchanged even in the face of the rupiah's depreciation. Similarly, energy price increases have been designed to protect low-volume users as much as possible. As a result of these measures the subsidy on fuel and electricity has increased to 2.9 per cent of GDP and 0.9 per cent of GDP respectively, while that for food has increased to about 1.5 per cent of GDP.

A critical aspect of the government's efforts to improve food security is the need to rehabilitate and strengthen the distribution system following the disruptions and damage caused by the social unrest in May 1998. While private trading appears to be returning to normal in many parts of the country, the government feels that additional temporary measures are required to further improve the distribution system. The Ministry of Industry and Trade has established a special monitoring unit to identify potential shortages of foodstuffs or distribution networks so that the government can take early corrective action. The government, in key parts of the country, has extended special security arrangements for the transportation of essential commodities. Retailing has suffered severe dislocation, and the government is trying to reactivate the retail network through the rehabilitation and construction of traditional markets. In some especially poor and remote regions of the country, where transport costs have risen sharply due to a shortage of spare parts, the government is considering providing facilities for the direct distribution of food by government agencies. The Ministry of Home Affairs has instructed regional governors and local authorities to mobilise support for the private retail and wholesale sector, including streamlining licensing procedures to facilitate inter-provincial trade.

The government is working closely with community-based groups to expand labour-intensive public works programmes, with the objective of increasing the incomes of the poor, the unemployed and the underemployed, and overall to enhance purchasing power in rural and urban areas. These programmes have moved to the top of the priority list, and their funding will be increased. To supplement these efforts, food-for-work programmes are also being implemented in drought-stricken areas of the country.

To ensure continued high enrolment rates for children through the first nine years of school, and hence to maintain the human capital stock of the country, a national campaign has been launched by the government. This includes a 5-year $US 380 million programme of scholarships for the poorest junior secondary students and special assistance funds (block grants) for the poorest primary and junior secondary schools, as well as coordinated mass media and interpersonal communications activities. It complements ongoing efforts to maintain existing levels of quality by providing textbooks, materials and in-service training. To sustain basic health care services the government has restructured its budget in order to finance essential drugs, including the vaccines and drugs needed for communicable disease control, targeted at the poor.

4.   Indonesia's economic and social prospects in the short to medium run

Economic prospects

Although the factors behind the Asian financial crisis are very similar for all of the affected East Asian economies, Indonesia's position is quite different. Its economic collapse is much deeper and more complex than for most of the other countries in the region, and political factors have compounded the difficulties of the country's programme of measures in response to the crisis. Table 7.3 summarizes prospective developments in the Indonesian economy during 1998 and 1999, as well as developments in 1996 and 1997. There was a general anticipation that GDP growth would be negative during the 1998–99 period, and would be particularly severe in 1998. Inflation has risen dramatically during 1998 and is anticipated to be 60 per cent for the year as a whole. The prospect of an 80 per cent

Table 7.3   Indonesia's short-term economic outlook, 1996–99

	1996	*1997*	*1998*	*1999*
Real GDP growth (%)	8.0	4.5	–14.0	–3.5
CPI (%)	7.9	6.6	60.0*	27.0*
Short term interest rates (%), end of period	13.3	28.5	60.0	na
Government budget balance % of GDP, end of period	1.0	1.2	–6.0	–6.0
Current account balance % of GDP	–3.3	–2.9	3.9	3.7
Foreign exchange reserves $US billion	24.0	20.5	20.5	26.5
External debt, % of GDP, end of period	55.4	62.4	181.5	188.6
Short term debt, $U.S billion	41.3	36.8	29.0	18.4

* The CPI rate of inflation was 72 per cent for the 12 months to July 1998 and is predicted to be 80 per cent for the 12 months to December 1998 falling to 27 per cent for the 12 months to December 1999.
Source: J. P. Morgan, *Asian Financial Markets*, Third Quarter, July 1998, p. 44.

rate of inflation by December 1998 is anticipated to abate considerably during 1999. Short-term interest rates have, not surprisingly, increased dramatically in line with the rapid increase in inflation, and were anticipated to rise to around 60 per cent by the end of 1998. The government's fiscal deficit was also anticipated to rise steeply in 1998 to around 6 per cent of GDP for the calendar year, and to remain at this for 1999. This is a reflection of the rising costs to the government of protecting the poor and getting the economy re-started, as well as weaknesses on the revenue side. The extent of such budget deficits is clearly unsustainable, but appropriate in the context of the economic crisis currently facing the country, and will depend crucially upon foreign financial assistance for its funding.

By the 1999/2000 budget the government will need to have in place a more efficient, selective, and targeted set of subsidy mechanisms.

The decline in the country's domestic income and expenditure can be expected to improve both the trade and current account deficits. The current account itself is anticipated to move into surplus during both 1998 and 1999. Foreign exchange reserves are anticipated to stabilize during 1998, and to increase in 1999 due to the improvement in the current account balance. The major difficulty, as clearly indicated in Table 7.3, relates to the massive increase in the country's external debt which was anticipated almost to treble in 1998 in comparison to its level in 1997, and further to deteriorate in 1999. The servicing of this debt, as well as the repayment of the debt itself, is denominated predominantly in foreign currency. This exerts a major drain on the country's resources, and hence the need to restructure this debt is paramount. From Table 7.3 this is anticipated to be successful 1998/1999 as the size of short-term debt falls assuming that the country, primarily the private sector, is able to reach agreement with its foreign creditors over extending the maturity of this debt.

The recovery of the Indonesian economy from its desperate economic plight will depend upon an overall strategy that involves stimulating demand through public spending, overcoming micro-economic deficiencies and which begins with the long job of improving governance and institutions. At the macroeconomic level, at least initially, the focus for Indonesia's economic recovery will be public-sector spending. Private demand within the economy has dramatically declined and will therefore need to be offset by a period of Keynesian pump priming. Current budget forecasts call for an 8.5 per cent budget deficit during financial year 1998/99, to be financed by increased external borrowing from official and concessional sources to avoid inflation. This budget deficit is likely to be the primary instrument that will halt the slide in Indonesia's domestic demand.

A number of microeconomic reforms will be needed as well, to ensure that Indonesian firms can compete internationally. These reforms include long needed improvements in regulations and processes affecting business in Indonesia, as well as structural repairs to damage caused by the economic and social shocks which the economy has sustained. The linkage between banks and corporations is the key challenge of the restructuring process. At current exchange rates, interest rates and market conditions, most Indonesian corporations and SMEs are bankrupt. In turn, most banks are insolvent as bad debts climb to unheard-of levels. As domestic demand dries up and regional export prospects dim, even exporters with potential markets, especially newcomers without established contacts, are hard pressed to take advantage of them, as trade and working capital finance has all but ceased to flow.

A medium-term strategy for Indonesia that embraces efforts to stimulate demand and which incorporates microeconomic and institutional reforms should consist of the following four elements:

- rebuilding the financial system and restarting the corporate sector;
- building on strengths: using agriculture and natural resources as leading sectors;
- priority investments in critical infrastructure;
- build and improve government institutions.

No economy can prosper without a functioning financial system, especially a banking system. Domestic savings and the credit it generates will be the cornerstone of Indonesian investment for the coming decade. The agriculture and natural resources sectors have been the traditional strengths of the economy, and these could be used once again as a launching pad for the recovery and future development of the economy. Economic recovery will also require the need to identify and develop core infrastructure which can form the basis of the government's publics works programme, although the financing of renewed investments in infrastructure in the aftermath of the crisis will pose formidable challenges and require foreign assistance. Indonesia's corporate sector and banks are unlikely to be willing, or able, to conduct such expenditure. Strengthening governance, both corporate and public sector, may be the single greatest challenge Indonesia faces in the coming decade. If Indonesia is ever to regain the confidence of international, and domestic, investors, it must build institutions and adopt regulations that meet international standards. At the core of the governance challenge lie two of Indonesia's most pervasive and most flawed systems, its legal system and its civil service system. The answer to reducing corruption is simple, transparency. In practice, Indonesia requires a shift in business culture, and this will require a clear and absolute commitment from the highest ranks of government, and a functioning legal system.

Taken together, these four elements will build a recovery pro-gramme that at once uses public-sector spending to augment demand, and at the same time improve productive capacities and create infrastructure and institutions to serve Indonesia in the coming decades. However, rebuilding the Indonesian economy will require effort by both the Indonesians and the international com-munity. This will require political stability and especially a political and legal climate that reassures domestic as well as international investors, and gives them confidence they are welcome and can operate safely.

Social impact and prospects

One of the most immediate challenges facing the Indonesian gov-ernment lies in the need to address the humanitarian challenges. As many as 50 million Indonesians face a return to poverty as a result of the drought and financial crisis according to the World Bank (1998c), which has called for international donors to support the government's efforts to feed the hungry, sustain health services for the sick, and keep a generation of children from dropping out of school. Based upon World Bank projections the social prospects for the country over the short to medium term look extremely bleak. At least 20 million people are expected to lose their jobs, with unemployment in Jakarta alone having risen by 21 per cent during May 1998 according to official figures. Ethnic trouble is likely to intensify under pressure from growing poverty, with effects that could include a disruption of the economic distribution system due to conflict in some urban areas. The Chinese community in particular appears to have been the primary target. Increased crime has occurred and is likely to increase as economic circumstances deteriorate. About 20 per cent of Indonesia's poorer children are at serious risk of dropping out of school as a response to shrinking family incomes. This will have a long-term deleterious effect upon the country's human capital stock, and a number of measures have been implemented with the objective of reversing this development, as discussed previously.

5. Summary and conclusions

It is clear that Indonesia is in a deep economic, financial, political and social crisis. A country that achieved decades of rapid growth, stability and poverty reduction is now near economic collapse. Within the space of one year Indonesia has seen its currency fall in value by 80 per cent, inflation soar to over 50 per cent, the economy swing from rapid growth to even more rapid contraction, unemployment climb rapidly, and the stock exchange lose much of its value. Foreign creditors have withdrawn and investors have retreated. Capital and entrepreneurs have fled. Long-standing defects in governance, earlier camouflaged by rapid growth, have now been unmasked as fatal flaws. Unfortunately, the crisis hit when Indonesia was experiencing its worst drought in 50 years, and the international oil price was registering a sharp decline. Social unrest has erupted and shaken to its very core, the political stability of the nation. Years of development and poverty reduction are at risk.

No country in recent history, let alone one the size of Indonesia, has ever suffered such a dramatic reversal of fortune. The next years will be difficult and uncertain. The economy was expected to contract in 1998 by 10–15 per cent and by a further 3.5 per cent in 1999, inflation could exceed 80 per cent by the end of 1998, and the number of poor could well double. These developments are of particular concern given that Indonesia is the world's fourth largest country, an important anchor of stability in East Asia, having had an impressive past record of development and social progress. Recovering from this desperate situation will be slow and difficult. Much will depend on whether the nation can achieve the necessary political stability for implementing a difficult and complex agenda of economic reforms, both at the macroeconomic and microeconomic levels, and whether it will receive the necessary financial support from the international community. The necessary agenda of action for the near term will require the concentrated focus of government policy and the full support of the international community. The latter is of considerable importance.

By mid 1998 there were clear signs that the international community was responding to Indonesia's plight. The country's international donors, amounting to more than thirty countries, pledged in July 1998 to back the government's commitment to extensive reform with $US 7.9 billion in disbursements for the Indonesian fiscal year 1998/99, which represented a significant increase over the previous year's figure. This amount, together with exceptional financing of more than $US 6 billion that has already been arranged, matches what is required to fill the 1998/99 budget gap identified in the Indonesian economic programme. This will be important in stabilizing the country, both economically and socially, over the short term, and provide an important platform for the recovery of the economy over the medium to long term.

Notes

1. The outcome of these upheavals led to the resignation of President Suharto and his replacement by President Habibie.
2. More than 40 per cent of Indonesia's external debt is denominated in yen.
3. This was primarily as a consequence of the impact of the social disturbances on the Chinese community, which appeared to be singled out for looting and other abuse. This section of the Indonesian community has experienced such difficulties in the past, and it is believed that much of this community's capital fled the country. This is of considerable economic significance, for although the Chinese community accounts for only 3 per cent of the total population it is estimated to control some 70 per cent of the country's financial wealth.
4. At mid-1998.

References

Australian Department of Foreign Affairs and Trade (1997), *Country Economic Brief – Indonesia*, Canberra, August.

Economist (The) (1998), *A Survey of East Asian Economies*, London, March.

Government of Indonesia (1998), Memorandum of Economic and Financial Policies, Jakarta, 15 January.

Government of Indonesia (1998), Supplementary Memorandum of Economic and Financial Policies, Jakarta, 10 April.

Government of Indonesia (1998), Second Supplementary Memorandum of Economic and Financial Policies, Jakarta, 24 June.

Government of Indonesia (1998), Indonesia statements of development policy: macroeconomic developments and economic reforms in Indonesia: a brief update, Jakarta, 2 July.

Harvie, C. (1999), 'Financial crisis in Indonesia: the role of good governance', in Tran Van Hoa and C. Harvie (eds), *The Causes and Impact of the Asian Financial Crisis*, Chapter 6, Macmillan, UK.

International Labour Organization (1998), *The Social Impact of the Asian Financial Crisis*, ILO Regional Office for Asia and the Pacific Basin, Bangkok, April.

International Monetary Fund (1998), *World Economic Outlook – Interim Assessment*, Washington, DC, May.

International Monetary Fund (1998), *World Economic Outlook*, Washington, DC, May.

World Bank (1998), Country brief: Indonesia, Washington, DC, July.

World Bank (1998a), *Indonesia's Road to Recovery*, Washington, DC, July.

World Bank (1998b), *Indonesia: resolving the crisis in the financial sector – a background note*, Washington, DC, July.

World Bank (1998c), *Addressing the Social Impact of the Crisis in Indonesia: a background note*, Washington, DC, July.

World Bank (1998d), *Indonesia in Crisis: a macroeconomic update*, Washington, DC, July.

8
Malaysia: Current Problems and Prospects to 2010

Frank Hiep Huynh

1. Brief review on the east Asian region

Serious questions have been raised about the future of the so-called 'miracle' economies in Asia such as Korea, Thailand, and to some extent the Philippines. The massive capital inflow was unprecedented during the last 10 years, amounting to about $US 1 trillion in 1996. The first sign of trouble revealed itself in July 1997 when Thailand was forced to devalue the baht. The ensuing International Monetary Fund (IMF) assistance was not completely welcome because it embodied severe operational conditionalities and cultural insensitivities, some of which are politically embarrassing to the local economies. In particular, the American economic dominance was openly denounced as a case of 'Pox America'. The view was widespread enough to make headlines in the Asian-Pacific Economic Cooperation (APEC) meeting in Vancouver in November 1997. In the wake of the currency crisis, there was a marked deterioration in the political desirability of economic openness. (Crone, 1998, Lloyd and Sawyer, 1997, and Suthad Setboonsarng, 1998, provide some excellent reviews.)

The following table presents some key economic summaries for Malaysia and Singapore for 1995 and 1996.

2. The driving force behind the crisis

It is well known that economic growth in the Association of South-East Asian Nations (ASEAN) group has been the fastest in the world

Table 8.1 Annual percentage growth rates : Malaysia and Singapore, 1996

	Malaysia		Singapore	
	1995	1996	1995	1996
Gross Domestic Product	9.5	8.6	8.8	7.0
Consumer Price Index	3.4	3.5	1.7	1.4
Fiscal Position as Percentage of GDP	3.2	3.7	6.1	5.9
Export	17.6	7.2	21.6	6.1
Current Account Deficit as percentage of GDP	−10.0	−4.9	16.9	15.0
1995 Per Capita Income ($US)	3890		26730	
Gross National Saving Rates (% of GNP)	36.4	38.8	49.9	49.7

Source: *ASEAN Macroeconomic Outlook,* Jakarta: ASEAN Academic Press, ASEAN Secretariat, 1998

during the last twenty-five years, averaging about 6.6 per cent annually, compared with an average of 3 per cent for the advanced economies for this period. Such macroeconomic growth gave little warning to the impending crisis. One of the causes is the ASEAN's system of fixed exchange rates which were pegged either partially or completely to the US dollar. Thus, when the dollar became stronger relative to the Japanese yen, the ASEAN currencies also strengthened, leading to a decrease in their exports, and to current account deficits. Further, the strength of economic development and international trade in the region also lead to increases in foreign borrowing. Of the $US 173 billion (consisting of cross-border claims (in all currencies) and local claims in non-local currencies (for ASEAN, except Singapore)), 60 per cent were from the non-bank private sector. In particular, the Malaysian non-bank private sector accounted for about 57 per cent of the country's total borrowing.

The ensuing expansion of loans was mainly channelled towards the real estate and motor car sectors, leading to the bubbles in these sectors. Following the collapse of the bubbles, the financial system severely suffered. Also apparent was the withdrawal of funds by international fund managers from the region to take advantage of the recovery of the Japanese yen in early 1997. The baht was forced to devalue on 2 July 1997; the contagion of depreciation then started to spread to the Philippines, Malaysia and Indonesia. For the period from 1 July 1997–24 January 1998, the total rate of decrease of the local currencies in terms of the US dollar was 83.6 per cent for the Indonesian rupiah, 44.9 for the Malaysian ringgit and 39.4 for the Philippine peso (Montes, 1998, Table U-1, p. xv).

Setboonsarng (1998) in his analysis emphasized two main causes of the crisis: (1) the general structural weakness of the economies in the region and (2) the risks factors inherent in the open capital and financial markets. In the first group, one can cite factors such as: low productivity and declining competitiveness, weakness in the financial sector (for example, inadequate supervision of the financial institutions, inadequate disclosure of financial transactions and reserves) and poor governance. These factors seem to support the well-known view of Krugman (1994) that growth in this region in Asia was due to increases in the utilization of inputs of production (labour and capital) rather than to increases in input productivity. That issue of Total Factor Productivity (TFP), an idea proposed by Larry Lau of Stanford University in the US early in the 1980s, is still hotly debated (see, for example, Wilson, 1995, and Dutta, 1996).

The second group reminds us of the natural features of the financial markets, namely the moral hazard, bubbles and herd instinct. Thus, it is possible to turn a local instability into a global one.

Over a very short time, the exchange rate crisis became a banking and financial crisis, then a crisis in the real sectors of four of the ASEAN countries, whose depreciated exchange rates also put pressure on the Singapore dollar. In particular, by July 1997 the Malaysian ringgit had depreciated by some 40 per cent. In general, interest rates were higher, slowing down the local manufacturing and industrial activities. On the unemployment front, the International Labour Organization (ILO) estimated that about 150,000 people have lost jobs in Malaysia alone.

The long-term damage to the economies in Asia and elsewhere is expected to be substantial, due to the decreased real income, increased import prices, and the reduced levels of health care, food, nutrition and education. The crisis was made worse by the El Nino weather phenomenon. Both are expected to cause long-term damage to the environment as the poor may be forced to exploit more natural resources.

Setboonsarng (1998) also identified several areas to be addressed as a result of the Asian crisis, such as the stabilization of the exchange rates; minimizing the social impact; strengthening the financial sector; greater involvement of the domestic private sector; adjustment of industrial structures, and reforming financial markets. But it is recognized that the ASEAN members should work closely together since each country is too small for the task. There are at least three aspects to be considered. First, the large size of the foreign debts has to be dealt with, and some new bankruptcy laws have to be devised. Second, the financial market has to be revitalized; some progress has been made by the establishment of a 'mutual monitoring system', as advocated by the IMF, in conjunction with Asian Development Bank. Third, the ASEAN economies should be revitalized by strengthening the ASEAN Free Trade Area (AFTA) in order to encourage intra-ASEAN trade.

On the other hand, the IMF rescue and reform packages have been criticized on at least three counts. First, the prescriptions ignored their impact on the local social conditions, for example, the recommendations of a quick removal of price controls in Indonesia have produced economic hardships, social unrest and political chaos with fatalities. Second, the IMF packages may have lent more protection to the international lenders than to the locals. Finally, the current local contraction may be amplified by the prescribed policies that have turned off credit to small and medium-sized businesses.

In this context, the Malaysian currency moved in September 1998 from a flexible to fixed exchange rate system will be of utmost interest. The following summary is based on a recent review by Ariff *et al.* (1998) which surveys the economy up to April 1998.

3. The Malaysian economy: overview of early 1998

Real gross domestic product (GDP) grew by around 7.6 per cent in 1997, but sentiments changed by the end of the year so that the prospects were not encouraging for 1998. In particular, real GDP was expected to grow by only 0.9 per cent for 1998. Most economic indicators were expected to show a downturn, and the only source of growth was expected to originate from the external sector. In particular, exports of goods and services would show a growth of 4.6 per cent, as opposed to a contraction of 3.3 per cent by imports. In nominal terms, the merchandise trade surplus was expected to reach a high of RM 28.2 billion in 1998. A small deficit of RM 1.1 billion was expected for the current account balance, or 0.4 per cent of GNP, a significant reduction relative to a deficit of RM 3.4 billion in 1997. Also the two indices (the business conditions index, and the consumer condition index) continued to show a downturn for the first quarter of 1998. Further, unemployment will remain a problem as the unemployment rate was expected to rise to 4.8 per cent in 1998, compared to a lower rate of 2.7 in 1997.

The commodities markets

Ariff *et al.* (1998) provide a review of several commodities such as palm oil, petroleum, liquified natural gas (LNG), rubber, tin, sawn logs and sawn timber. In general, the devaluation of the Malaysian ringgit has helped to increase exports for most of these categories. Export value for palm oil shows a rise of 14.6 per cent, the largest export receipt ever recorded, or a 4.9 per cent of total gross exports for 1997. On the other hand, petroleum shows a decrease of 2.0 per cent in export value. But export earnings for LNG rose by a favourable 42.3 per cent for the year, due to a rise in both volume and price. In contrast, a fall in rubber demand dictated a drop in earnings for rubber exports of 15.4 per cent (the rubber price was quoted in terms of the ringgit). It has been predicted that unit prices will remain weak due to strong competition from the surrounding economies in the region. As far as tin is concerned, the weaker ringgit helped to boost export earnings, with revenue rising by 18.9 per cent in the early months of 1998. Lastly, export receipt for both saw logs and sawn timber exhibited a decline of 0.3 per cent and 7.5 per cent respectively in the early months of 1998, although more favourable market conditions are predicted.

The industrial sector

This sector is covered by the Index of Industrial Production (IIP) which shows a small decrease from 11.0 per cent in 1996 to

10.7 in 1997. In the first half of 1997, the manufacturing division (accounting for some 70 per cent of the sector) remained strong but weakened in the second half. The export-oriented division of the sector showed slightly more strength, giving a 10.5 per cent growth in 1997 compared to 8.2 in 1996. This may have been helped by the depreciation of the ringgit. Similarly, the strong growth in the first half of 1997 of the textile and clothing industry was dampened in the second half of the year, due to the rising cost of raw materials. Further, the wood and wood products industry was one of the worst hit, due to the sharp downturn of the property sector.

A serious fall in the number of approved projects in the manufacturing sector occurred with a 3.6 per cent decline (to 754 from 782 in 1996), according to the Malaysian Industrial Development Authority (MIDA), leading to a sharp dip from RM 34.3 billion to RM 25.8 billion, or a decrease of 24.8 per cent. Nevertheless, the top three industries remain the petroleum, electrical and electronics, and basic metal products sectors, accounting for 64 per cent of total capital investment.

The banking system and monetary developments

From a growth rate of 28.4 per cent in October 1997, the loans and advances by the banking system slowed down slightly to 26.9 per cent. In value terms, a decline from RM 405.4 billion in December 1997 to RM 400.7 was recorded in January 1998.

In general, the monetary supply shows a moderate decline in all three measures of money supply (M1, M2 or M3). On the other hand the interest rate continued to increase; for example the 3-month interest rate rose from 9.1 in December 1997 to 9.35 a month later, due to the tight policy of the central bank. Reflecting the general increase in the cost of funds, the base lending rate of commercial banks also increased. If the inflation rate was to be about 7–8 per cent, the nominal interest rate would have to be around 11–12 per cent, but with the slowing down becoming clearer, a decrease in the interest rate is to expected.

Most alarming was the decline in the exchange rate of the ringgit which went to an all-time low of 4.88 against the US dollar in early January 1998. As reported below, the rate would be fixed at 3.8 when the central bank, Bank Negara, introduced currency controls.

Consumer and producer prices

The average inflation rate was 2.7 per cent for 1997, with monthly rates of 2.7, 2.6 and 2.9 per cent for October, November and December respectively. For the early months of 1998 the rate was expected to be higher by some two percentage points; one aggravating factor was the depreciation of the ringgit.

The prices paid by importers, as reflected by the Producer Price Index (PPI) showed an upward trend, surging from an annual rate of 1.7 per cent in August 1997 to 16 per cent in January of 1998. Among the items composing the index, the animal and vegetable oil indicated a large increase of 61.1 per cent, compared to only 8.7 per cent a year ago. Similarly, the prices charged by domestic producers were 21.8 per cent higher, and import prices went up by 16.1 per cent.

The cumulative trade surplus for January and February 1998 amounted to RM 5.1 billion, compared to RM 265.6 million for the corresponding period a year earlier. Further, the depreciated ringgit has induced a large increase in exports and imports when the figures were converted from the US dollar to the local ringgit; exports and imports showed a growth of nearly 50 per cent and 43 per cent respectively for the January–February period.

Other aspects of development

According to the Asian Development Bank (1997) the outlook for the economy 'in the next two years remains upbeat'; it forecast that the growth of the economy is likely to be underpinned by growth in domestic demand, particularly in public investment and consumption spending. Special mention was made of the fast implementation of the Kuala Lumpur International Airport and the Commonwealth Games village. The seventh Malaysian Plan (1996–2000) and the Industrial Master Plan, both approved in 1996, underpin a strategy based on productivity-driven growth, with particular emphasis on the development of human resources.

Another important project is the so-called Multimedia Super Corridor (MSC) which is envisaged to be the information hub for the region. Conceived and launched by the Prime Minister himself, the RM 5 billion corridor is a specially zoned 15 km by 40 km region South of Kuala Lumpur, and is intended as an industrial park for Information Technology (IT) companies. The corridor is expected to attract a large number of investors thanks to its location at the centre of ASEAN, to its competitive cost advantage, to the absence of entrenched interests partly due to its newness, and finally to the good track record of Malaysia in meeting its commitments.

Currency controls

In September 1998 the Central Bank of Malaysia, Bank Negara, issued a statement that read 'the Government of Malaysia has decided effective today, 1 September 1998, to implement a series of measures to insulate the Malaysian economy from the risks and vulnerability of [such] external developments'. The ringgit was then pegged at 3.8 to the US dollar, while the prevailing rate was around 4.2. Two months earlier, on 14 July 1998, the Bank had given up the defence of the ringgit

But unlike Thailand, Korea and the Philippines, Malaysia did not seek assistance from the IMF but instead imposed similar steps herself; one major reason for the policy move was the desperate need for foreign exchanges; but equally important is the fact that an involvement with the IMF would have forced the government to commit to a reform programme with severe repercussions on the native community, by closing down many of the bumiputra-owned companies and institutions.

The main changes in the exchange control policy apply to such items as:

(1) the external accounts (approval is required for transfers of funds),
(2) authorized depositary institutions (for purchases and sales of ringgit financial assets),
(3) trade settlements (all settlements are to be made in foreign currency), and
(4) limits on the amount of foreign currency held by travellers (a maximum of RM 1000 per person; no limit on the import of foreign currencies; export of foreign currencies limited to a maximum of RM 10 000).

The new policy is a brave one, given the dilemma of choices between either:

(1) tight fiscal policies (which would worsen the recession), or
(2) tight monetary policies (which would lead to more bad debts and threaten the financial institutions).

On the other hand, to adopt both kinds of policy would lead to further devaluation of the ringgit and asset deflation. The adopted currency option appears to be similar to option B advocated by Krugman; to make it work, other major reforms should also be made in areas such as regulatory procedures, legal infrastructure, transparency and enforcement.

The political environment is also not so good, due to the apparent disagreement between the Prime Minister, Dr Mahathir Mohamad, and his then deputy, Mr Anwar Ibrahim, who happened to be in favour of a free-enterprise model of the economy. Perhaps the sacking of Mr Anwar, then his imprisonment and the profound change in economic policies are all of the same political strategy.

4.   Apec and other regional commitments

Kuala Lumpur was to play host to APEC (Asian Pacific Economic Cooperation) in November 1998. The jailing of Anwar Ibrahim had already antagonized some country participants. But this problem aside, the meeting was a good chance for consolidation in the face of the threat of inward-looking regionalism in the wake of the European Union (EU) and the North America Free Trade Area (NAFTA) both of which are discriminatory and have intentions of enlargement (Yuan Tsao Lee, 1996). (Editor's note: At this meeting, Malaysia's currency controls and Japan's refusal to liberalize its fishing and forest products were attacked. An Asian-only version of APEC was proposed by Dr Mahathir).

5.   Conclusions

During the past two years, Thailand, the Philippines and Korea had experienced serious economic downturn and accepted revival packages from the IMF; on the other hand, Malaysia went her own way by initiating currency controls. It remains to be seen whether the Malaysian policy works; equally as important is the question of how long the economy will take to resurge under the new system. Another question of utmost interest is whether the Malaysian government has the wisdom and courage to abandon economic controls and return to a freer environment. At the moment, it appears that Dr Mahathir's approach has reasonable support and trust both within and outside Malaysia.

While we originally wished to look further ahead to the year 2010, the reality is, alas, imposing more constraints than we expected. In sum, the next two or three years will be crucial for Malaysia. The prospects for Malaysia to 2010 depend very much on what will happen to the country and its development and growth in the next two or three years in the context of economic globalization.

References

Ariff, Mohamed , *et al.* (1998) 'Malaysian Economic Outlook, 1998–99, 1st Quarter 1998 Update'. Kuala Lumpur: The Malaysian Institute of Economic Research.

Donald Crone (1998), 'Southeast Asia: A year when high ambition was challenged', *Southeast Asian Affairs*, 1998, 3–17. Singapore: Institute of Southeast Asian Studies.

Dutta, M. (1996) 'The New Industrial Revolution in Asian Economies : Has It Reached its Ceiling? – Some Remarks', *Journal of Asian Economics*, Vol. 7, No. 3, pp. 357–364.

Krugman, Paul (1994) 'The Myth of Asia's Miracle', *Foreign Affairs*, Vol. 73, No. 6, pp.62–78.

Lloyd, Peter J. and Kim R. Sawyer (1997) 'The Asian Economic and Financial Crisis: The Effects of Market Integration and Market Fragility', *Quarterly Bulletin of Economic Trends*, No. 4. University of Melbourne.

Montes, Manual F. (1998), *The Currency Crisis in Southeast Asia* (Updated Edition). Singapore: Institute of Southeast Asian Studies

Suthad Setboonsarng (1998), 'ASEAN Economic Cooperation: Adjusting to the Crisis', *Southeast Asian Affairs,* 1998, 18–36. Singapore: Institute of Southeast Asian Studies.

Yuan Tsao Lee (1996) 'APEC 1996: An ASEAN Perspective', *Journal of Asian Economics*, Vol. 7 , No. 2.

Wilson, Peter (1995) 'Sources of Economic Growth and Development in ASEAN: Closing and Summing Up', *Singapore Economic Review*, Vol. 40, No. 2, 237–253.

9
Foreign Trade of Asian Transitional Countries and Regions: World Competitiveness and its Development

Zhao Yanyun and Li Jingping

1. Introduction

The economic development of transitional countries and regions has played an important role in world economic development. The transitional economies, in fact, include two groups of countries and regions. One includes those developing economies that have practised a market economy and are transiting to the status of a newly industrialized economy. This kind of transition began in the 1970s, achieved great success in the 1980s and 1990s and, as a result, the countries involved are now called newly industrialized countries (NICs) and regions. In Asia, such countries includes Singapore, Hong Kong (China), Korea, and Taiwan (China), and they were classified as advanced economies by the International Monetary Fund (IMF) in May 1997 because they have such powerful world competitiveness. The other group of countries includes those economies that have practised a planned economy and are transiting to a market economy overall. This kind of transition began in the 1980s and China is a successful representative. From the viewpoint of development, the latter transition will involve the contents of the former. Asia has become the convergent region of successful transitional economies because it fits the needs of economic globalization and the information technology revolution, and has become the most competitive region in the world at least up to mid 1997.

This chapter tries to analyse world competitiveness and the development of foreign trade in some major Asian transitional countries and regions from this viewpoint.

2.   Asia's economic development and world competitiveness

The economic development and world competitiveness of Asia have entered an important stage. From the overall ranks of world competitiveness, we find that the Asian countries have very strong competitive advantages, and they are all transitional economies except for Japan. In terms of economic development and world competitiveness, the Asian transitional economies can be classified into three levels: the first includes the NICs and regions, that is, Hong Kong (China), Taiwan (China), Singapore, and Korea; the second includes newly developing countries, or those countries with an accelerating growth, that is, Malaysia, Indonesia, Thailand and the Philippines; the third includes those countries that have been pushed forward by reforms and opening-up, that is, China, India and Vietnam. These three levels are strengthening the cooperation and development, adapting the economic globalization process and the information technology revolution, and overcoming the temporary difficulties caused by the 1997 Asian financial crisis. From all these developments we can see that a basic tendency of all Asian economies to transition has formed, and Asian competitiveness is thus an important issue for analysis and discussion.

3.   World competitiveness and development of foreign trade of the NICS

The characteristics of the strengthening of world competitiveness

The world is fixing its eyes on the development of Asian NICs. These countries have achieved a great success in the process of adapting economic globalization and the information technology revolution, and have formed a strong world competitiveness ranking. The characteristics of the strengthening of world competitiveness can be summarized as follows:

1. The Asian NICs have emphasized the culture and development of their domestic economies. Most of these countries and regions have a strong domestic economy. For example, Singapore is ranked second among 46 major countries and regions in the world. In fact, strengthening its domestic economy is the essential starting-point for a country to improve its world competitiveness. A strong domestic economy is embodied in a strong ability to create value-added, high domestic saving and investment, appropriate consumption demands, coordinated growths among the industries and low living costs. The ability of creating value-added is embodied in the high growth rate of the GDP and the GDP per capita. For example, among the 10 countries and regions with the highest real GDP growth rate in the world in 1996, eight countries and regions were from Asia and their growth rates were all higher than 6.7 per cent. Among the 10 countries and regions with the highest real GDP per capita growth rate in the world in 1996, nine countries and regions were from Asia.

2. The Asian NICs have deepened the opening-up policy and improved management. To deepen the opening-up is to deepen the internationalization policy. Internationalization is the necessary condition for each country to compete in trade in the world, to promote the development process, to improve the domestic economy, and to strengthen its ability to create value-added. However, internationalization must be integrated with an effective management which includes government management, the financial system and enterprise management. The Asian NICs and regions, except Korea, all have an effective government management, a sound (till 1997) financial system and a flexible enterprise management. In fact, if one country can fully utilize the internationalization process, government management, financial systems, and enterprise management, and introduce other subjective initiatives well, this has the effect of strengthening the domestic economy and speeding up its economic growth.

3. The Asian NICs have speeded up the construction of infrastructure, improved the quality of science and technology and their people, and established a good basis for achieving world competitiveness. The above-mentioned bases of Asian NICs and regions are weak, but they have fully realized the important role of these bases to improve their world competitiveness, and they have been dedicated to improving it by creating the necessary conditions. For example, the infrastructure of Singapore has been vastly improved. Its infrastructure was ranked 11 in 1997, which rose 17 ranks compared with the rank of 28 in 1992. Its science and technology and people also ranked well: 8 and 5 respectively.

4. The Asian NICS have emphasized the attractiveness and aggressiveness of their policies. On the world scene, a country should effectively and fully make use of the international capital market. It should not only attract, but also aggress. While keeping the balance between these two aspects, it will promote its world competitiveness and the development of foreign trade. The Asian NICs and regions have emphasized the use of the flow of international capital in order to develop their domestic economy. They have had not only successful experiences, but also some lessons from failures. The current Asian financial crisis is one such lesson.

The competitiveness of foreign trade

The competitiveness of foreign trade is an important part of world competitiveness. It can be measured by trade performance competitiveness, imports and exports, the structure of foreign trade, development tendency and potential, and the effects of foreign trade on the domestic economy. The Asian transitional countries and regions have a strong competitiveness in foreign trade. The share of GDP of the 11 transitional economies (Singapore, Hong Kong [China], Taiwan [China], Korea, Malaysia, Indonesia, Thailand, the Philippines, China, India, and Vietnam) in the world is only 9.3 per cent, while the share of exports of these 11 countries in the world is 17.1 per cent. Their real export growth rates are rather high. In the annual assessment made by the World Economic Forum (WEF), from June 1996 to June 1997, exports had greatly enhanced the

domestic economic developments of the Asian transitional countries and regions. Since 1992 the Institute for Management
Development (IMD) in Switzerland has made a continuous assessment of each of these countries' competitiveness in trade performance and in exports and imports of goods and services. According to
the assessment, China, Hong Kong and Malaysia have a very strong
competitiveness, and Korea, Thailand and Taiwan (China) also have
a rather strong competitiveness. But on the whole, the Asian transitional economies all have some other serious problems. These
include the serious imbalance within the competitiveness of foreign
trade, relatively less serious problems in trade performance competitiveness, the imbalance of the trade account, bad trade conditions,
the unstable foreign exchange rates, and so on. The imbalance of
development between imports and exports also exists in some countries and regions. We will discuss the problems in the competitiveness of foreign trade of some Asian NICs and regions in more detail
below.

The problems in the competitiveness of foreign trade

1. Singapore is one of the most powerfully competitive countries
    in the world. It surpassed Japan in this respect in 1994 and
    ranked second only to the US, and this situation was been
    maintained until 1997. Meanwhile, its competitiveness of
    foreign trade is also very strong. Its competitiveness in trade
    performance and in exports of goods and services both ranked
    first among 46 major countries in 1996. But its competitiveness
    of foreign trade changed in 1997. Both this and the import of
    goods and services competitiveness have been weakened since.
    The causes of this weaker trade performance competitiveness
    lie in the following factors: the stability of the foreign
    exchange rate which dropped from rank 15 in 1996 to rank 24
    in 1997; the considerable, serious imbalance of the trade
    account; the unfavourable trade conditions. The major cause of
    the weaker imports of goods and services competitiveness lies
    in a slower growth rate of imports which dropped from rank 7
    in 1996 to rank 15 in 1997. In conclusion, the unstable foreign
    exchange rate and the slower growth rate of imports are the
    most important problems for Singapore's competitiveness in
    foreign trade.

2. Hong Kong is also one of the most powerfully competitive countries and regions in the world and it has maintained rank 3 since 1994. Its trade performance competitiveness has been considerably weak, and the competitiveness of its imports of goods and services was weakened in 1997 compared with that in previous years. The major cause of a weak trade performance competitiveness lies in the imbalance of the current account, and where the deficit of the trade account is large. The major cause of a weaker imports of goods and services competitiveness lies in the slower growth rate of imports which dropped from rank 12 in 1996 to rank 24 in 1997. In conclusion, the imbalance of the current account and the slower growth rate of imports are the most important problems for Hong Kong's competitiveness in foreign trade.

3. Taiwan (China) is one of the most powerfully competitive countries and regions in Asia. Its world competitiveness dropped from rank 18 in 1996 to rank 23 in 1997, and its competitiveness in foreign trade was also weakened in 1997. The major problems are that the competitiveness of both exports and imports of goods and services was weakened. However, its trade performance competitiveness has since been improved and its balance of payments is in good condition.

4. The world competitiveness of Korea is below the average level. The characteristics of Korea's world competitiveness are that it has been keeping a powerful domestic economy, but it lacks the competitiveness of foreign trade. In 1997 its trade performance competitiveness was weakened considerably: the competitiveness of the balance of the current account ranked 43 among 46 countries and regions; the competitiveness of the stability of the foreign exchange rate ranked 35. At the same time, the imports of goods and services competitiveness was also weakened considerably. In conclusion, the imbalance of payments and the unstability of the foreign exchange rate are the most important problems for Korea's competitiveness in foreign trade.

4. Analysis of the competitiveness of foreign trade

As a whole, the fundamental problem of the Asian NICs and regions is their imbalance in the development of foreign trade competitiveness. It is embodied in the following factors: the imbalance between the development of imports and exports; the imbalance of the trade account; the weakening trade conditions; the unstable foreign exchange rate. At the time of the information technology revolution and the upgrading of industrial structure, the big international league of nations with large imports and exports is the most important driving force for the global economy. Each country must adapt itself to the development of new technologies, pursue the stability of the whole economy and maintain the economic structure on a flexible and systematic basis. We have calculated the correlation coefficients between world competitiveness and all its determining factors, and found that the coefficients between world competitiveness and management and finance are the highest, respectively at 0.9362 and 0.9165. We have also calculated the correlation coefficients between the determining factors, and found that the coefficient between internationalization and finance is high. So, we can draw a conclusion that finance has important effects on both the world competitiveness and the foreign trade competitiveness one country or region. Many Asian NICs and regions lost their finance competitiveness in 1997: Singapore dropped two ranks; Hong Kong, five; Taiwan, two; Korea, three. And the competitiveness of Korea's finance is the worst: its ranking was 43.

The finance competitiveness includes the cost and availability of capital, stock market dynamism and banking sector efficiency. These four sub-factors in Singapore ranked respectively 10, 8, 4 and 5 among the 46 countries and regions in 1997. Although these ranks are rather good, three of them, except the rank of stock market dynamism, dropped when compared with the situation in 1992. The four ranks of Hong Kong had continued to drop during this period. Compared with the situation in 1996, the ranks of the cost of capital and banking sector efficiency dropped considerably in 1997, by 9 and 12 ranks respectively. The finance competitiveness of Taiwan (China) is weak: three ranks, except the rank of banking sector efficiency, dropped, especially the rank of availability of capital which ranked 34. Korea's finance competitiveness is the worst among these four economies, and its ranks of the availability of capital and banking sector efficiency have been kept the lowest in the world. So, we can conclude that the weak and declining finance competitiveness directly determines the foreign trade competitiveness of many Asian NICs and regions.

5.   Foreign trade competitiveness in Thailand, Malaysia, Indonesia and the Philippines

The problems of the foreign trade competitiveness of Thailand, Malaysia, Indonesia and the Philippines are similar to that of the previous four economies, that is, they did not efficiently improve their finance competitiveness while improving their foreign trade competitiveness, so the finance sector does not become the powerful driving force to their long-term economic development. Besides, these countries' infrastructure, people, science and technology, and management all lack competitiveness. These four factors also have effects on foreign trade competitiveness to some extent. Because some of the Asian countries and regions lack a finance competitiveness, and their financial development does not coordinate with their economic development, the financial crisis broke out at last. The financial sector hinders not only economic development, but also the development of foreign trade competitiveness, and the competitiveness of exports, imports, the balance of payments and the foreign exchange rate will be subsequently weakened.

6.   China's development of world and foreign trade competitivenesses

The success of economic reform and opening-up in China

China's economic reform and opening-up policy have achieved great successes, and these have been acknowledged world wide. The overall rank of its world competitiveness was the best among the transitional countries as assessed by the WEF and the IMD in 1993. Since it was formally assessed in 1994, China's world competitiveness has been significantly improved. Take the world competitiveness as of 1997 as an example, 63 major competitiveness indicators ranked above 14 in the world, and 47 indicators ranked above 10. China has a very strong domestic economy, especially in terms of those indicators that reflect growth. China's internationalization has made great progress, ranking 29 in 1997 as againts 41 in 1994, and its introduction and utilization of foreign funds have a special competitiveness in the world. Chinese government management has been keeping a strong competitiveness, and this competitiveness has continued to improve, ranking 6 in 1997 compared to 14 in 1994. On the other hand, the finance, infrastructure, management and people (human resource) sectors all lack competitiveness. In this sectors they ranked among the lower-ranked countries in the world. However, with the reform and opening-up policy in recent years, these four factors' competitiveness as well that of science and technology are being improved. In conclusion, China's world competitiveness is growing rapidly, and its future status will surely attract the world's attention.

Chinese foreign trade competitiveness

Since it was formally assessed in 1994, China's foreign trade competitiveness has been improved to some extent. Its competitiveness in trade performance and imports of goods and services has improved, but that in exports of goods and services is weak. China's exports competitiveness ranks higher than 40 among 46 economies, and the major problems lie in the following factors: the ratio of exports to GDP is quite low; the diversity of exports is weak; the factoring is too small; the ratio of high-tech product exports to total exports is too low. The improvement of imports competitiveness has been directly connected to China's thinking highly of its attractiveness and importance. China is one of those countries that utilize foreign funds most. Finally, since China's trade account is in good condition, its trade performance competitiveness is considerably strong as a result.

The basis of China's foreign trade competitiveness is not very good. Its finance competitiveness ranked 40 in 1997, and the competitiveness of the availability of capital ranked 43, which will probably hinder more than help the development of Chinese foreign trade competitiveness. In addition, China's infrastructure and management also lack competitiveness. The above-mentioned situations show that the basis of China's foreign trade competitiveness is not solid. However, the Chinese government and science and technology sectors have quite a high competitiveness. Efficient government management may have ensured the smooth development of reform and opening-up policies, which will promote the overall progress of China's world competitiveness. Meanwhile, an efficient government management will help to formulate rational economic policies, which will forcefully push the economy forward. The

Southeast Asian financial crisis has left China with only a slight, unfavourable contagion, but much useful enlightenment. So far, China has established a financial risk consciousness and strengthened the preventing measures, so, it will surely improve its finance competitiveness in order to adapt to the needs of its economic development.

Analysis of the growth of China's foreign trade competitiveness

China has been transiting to a market economy since 1990, and the growth of Chinese foreign trade competitiveness has been good. The annual growth rate of Chinese foreign trade is high, the balance of trade account is improving, and the domestic economy is continuously strengthened. But there exist substantial fluctuations in the growth of Chinese foreign trade competitiveness: the growth of total imports and exports reached the lowest point in 1996, and it climbed up significantly in 1997. Generally, Chinese foreign trade competitiveness is entering a good period for growth.

There are four years in which the growth rate of Chinese exports exceeded 20 per cent: 1987, 1994, 1995 and 1997. From the viewpoint of development, the trend of the growth rate of Chinese exports is one of strengthening. The major causes for this include:

(1) China's economic reform is deepened step by step and the strategy of efficiently reallocating capital was carried out, thus improving the competitiveness of large and medium state-owned enterprises and therefore, the growth of exports has been enhanced.

(2) The science and technology structural reform has improved Chinese science and technology competitiveness. Especially, the connection of science and technology capital to industrial capital has pushed the growth of high-tech industries, the renewal of traditional industries, and management innovations. As a result, the exports of high-tech products and production technology have been enhanced.

(3) The growth of foreign-fund-owned enterprises has strengthened Chinese exports.

(4) The strategy of diversifying the export markets was carried out, which has greatly promoted the growth of Chinese exports.

(5) China is expanding its exports to the regions besides Asia, especially to Africa.

The growth rate of Chinese imports was only 2.5 per cent in 1997, which is the slowest since 1990. The major causes for this include:

(1) Chinese import substitution was strengthened and the market share of domestic products was rising;
(2) the domestic consumer demand was soft, so the demand to imported products was declining;
(3) the growth rate of investment was slowing, so the demand to imported products was decreased.

7.   The influences of the Asian financial crisis on the development of China's foreign trade competitiveness

The influences on Chinese imports and exports

Because of the Asian financial crisis, some sectors in China have reported that their imports and exports began to diminish from July 1997, but most of them said the extent was not very deep. After we adjusted for the seasonal cycle, the cyclical fluctuations and the random fluctuations on the basis of the monthly time series of exports, we were able to observe better the trend of exports. We find that Chinese exports have been continuously declining since July 1997. So, we can draw some tentative deductions that the Asian financial crisis has begun to influence China's economy. More details are given below:

1.   According to the statistics from the Chinese Customs Head-office, the growth rate of exports from China to the East Asian economies had decreased month by month in the last quarter of 1997, from 34.07 per cent in September to 6.84 per cent in December; the growth rate of exports from China to Japan and Korea was negative, respectively from 2.24 per cent and 39.07 per cent in September to –9.96 per cent and –6.47 per cent in December. The total exports to these regions decreased by $US 0.53 billion in December compared with that of September.

2.   The exports from China to the East Asian economies have decreased since early 1998. Some Chinese foreign trade companies have reported that the orders from Southeast Asian countries and Korea have been considerably reduced. In fact, some

companies have not received any order from these countries since 1997. For example, the Shanghai Pudong Steel Group Company (SPSGC) exported 40 thousand tons of steel from January to June in 1997, which increased four times more than the same period in 1996. But in the second half of 1997, the price of steel in the Southeast Asian countries' local markets reduced to $290 from $320 due to the devaluation of their currencies, so all the deliveries from SPSGC in the second part of 1997 were the orders received in the first part of the year, not new orders.

3. Some contracts that have passed the negotiation stage still cannot be signed. For example, the Shanghai Electricity and Gas Imports and Exports Group Company planned to export electronic stations to the Philippines, which had negotiated for four years and had decided to sign in November 1997, but now, this contract has been deferred indefinitely.

4. The product prices of Southeast Asian countries and Korea have greatly fallen due to the devaluation of their currencies caused by the financial crisis, so the competitiveness of Chinese export products has been weakened. For example, because the foreign exchange rate of the Korean won (KRW) has dropped from KRW800/$US to KRW1800/$US , the price of chrome-nickel steel has reduced from $US 320/ton to $US 160/ton, so the steel products of the Shanghai Baoshan Steel Company cannot enter the Korean market. Another example is: Southeast Asia is one of the most important sale markets for cement in the world, and specifically so for China. The international price of cement has, however, reduced by 20 per cent and more, due to the financial crisis, so China has lost the price competitiveness of cement, and its market share is being threatened. Under this situation, some cement factories have reduced or stopped production in the Shandong and Jiangxi provinces.

The influences on Chinese attractiveness to foreign funds

Hong Kong, Taiwan, Korea and Southeast Asian countries are the major countries and regions for China to attract foreign direct investment (FDI) from. The FDI from these regions comprised

61 per cent of the total real utilization of FDI into China in 1996, and comprised more than 80 per cent if we include those investments from Japan. The financial crisis has weakened the ability of these regions' investors, so FDI to China has been adversely influenced. According to the official statistics, China really utilized $US 62 billion in 1997, at the growth rate of 13 per cent. This pace is nearly equal to that of the previous year. If analysing the issue in more detail, we can find that the negotiated value of FDI has reduced somewhat, but the rate of contract implementation had risen somewhat in 1997, so the influence on Chinese attractiveness to foreign funds in 1997 as caused by the Asian financial crisis has not been very obvious or clear.

The influence on Chinese attractiveness to FDI in 1998 may become more obvious, so the Chinese government has to pay much attention to this influence and has developed a number of policies to deal with the situation. First, the Chinese government has reintroduced a favourable policy on the machinery imported by foreign-fund-owned enterprises. This policy will on the one hand encourage foreign-fund-owned enterprises to import more machinery (this policy was carried out in 1996, and the growth rate of imported machinery reached 32.6 per cent that year), but on the other hand, it will attract more FDI. Second, the Chinese government has expanded the scale of domestic investment, especially the investment on infrastructure, energy and raw materials. In addition, the investment in the high-tech industry led by the proliferation of information technology revolutions and innovations will increase, too. The rapid growth of domestic investment will also promote FDI.

The influence of the Chinese currency on foreign exchange

The foreign exchange rate of the Chinese yuan (CNY) has been kept stable in general. Under the situation that the difference between supply and demand conditions continues to expand, the CNY appreciated by 2.2 per cent against the US dollar in 1997, which was lower than the expected 2.4 per cent. China has begun to compile the nominal effective exchange rate index from January 1996. The index is in fact a trade weighted index: it sets the nominal effective exchange rate of the CNY in 1994 as 100, selects the foreign exchange rates of the currencies of 20 countries (these countries' total imports [from] and exports to China have the greatest share of total trade) against the CNY, and calculates on the basis of the weights of each country's total trade value with China. The index for January, June and December in 1996 was, respectively, 105.82 per cent, 107.16 per cent and 109.08 per cent. So the change was fairly stable and the appreciation was small in these years. The index rose to 121.96 per cent in December 1997 and rose by 13.88 per cent in 1998. From the monthly index, we can find that the index rose most rapidly in November and December in 1997, rising respectively 3.03 per cent and 3.93 per cent. This means that the magnitude of the appreciation in 1997 was much larger than that of 1996.

Because the foreign exchange rates of the Southeast Asian currencies and the KRW dropped one after another, the Chinese government has had to pay much attention to the trend of the CNY's foreign exchange rates. China's foreign exchange reserves reached $US 140 billion at the end of 1997, which was $US 40 billion more than that of 1996, so China has considerable ability to prevent a financial crisis or contagion from other Asian economies. Meanwhile, China is further strengthening its financial regulations, expanding exports, increasing investment and reinforcing the adjustment and management of the foreign exchange fluctuations. All these will surely help to prevent a crisis happening in China or to minimize the impact of the Asian economic turmoil on China in the next few years.

10
China: East Asia's Next Economic Domino?

Charles Harvie

1. Introduction

During its reform era China has experienced, and become accustomed to, high rates of economic growth, and rapid employment growth particularly in the rural collectives and, more recently, private enterprises. Strong fixed-asset investment and consumer demand in conjunction with a strong growth of net exports, provided the foundations for this. However, during the latter part of 1997, after four years of monetary austerity measures, there were worrying signs that the growth of the economy was slowing considerably, primarily from a weakening of consumer and investment demand. The growth of net exports, however, remained buoyant during 1997, but this has become increasingly threatened by the intensification of the financial crisis afflicting other East Asian economies during 1998.

Such developments, both internal and external, are of particular concern to China where the maintenance of employment growth, for its rapidly expanding workforce, and social cohesion is seen as being paramount. It is widely perceived that the country must keep growth above 7–8 per cent[1] if enough new jobs are to be created to absorb the rising unemployed as well as new entrants into the labour force, and that without appropriate action by the authorities the economy will be dangerously close to this in the foreseeable future. The current economic slowdown will also threaten the government's attempts to implement badly needed restructuring of the country's state-owned enterprises (SOEs) as well as the debt-laden state banks. It will also have broader adverse implications for other Asian nations attempting to export their way out of their financial difficulties, arising from the financial and economic crisis in the region. China's policymakers therefore currently face a severe problem of deflation rather than inflation. Of particular concern to China's neighbours, and indeed to the global economy, is the prospect that this deflation could be sufficiently strong that the authorities feel obliged to devalue the renminbi (RMB) as a means of regaining international competitiveness and stimulating export growth. This would have major adverse consequences for stability of both the regional and indeed global economies. The policy response to these difficulties will need to be innovative and unlike that used in the past, as China has become a quite different economy during its period of reform. In addition the country has become a significant regional economic player, and this too will have an important bearing upon its policy response. It is towards an analysis of these issues that this chapter is directed.

The chapter proceeds as follows. Section 2 identifies the ways in which the Asian financial crisis has impacted on the Chinese economy. Section 3 analyses the likelihood that China will devalue its currency as a result of its economic downturn and loss of competitiveness to its regional neighbours. China's prospective role as an engine of growth in the region as well as a potential harbinger of regional instability arising from its own internal difficulties is discussed in section 4. Section 5 critically analyses and evaluates the government's policy response to the economy's deteriorating performance, with the objective of increasing growth and expanding employment opportunities while maintaining low inflation. Finally section 6 provides a summary of the major conclusions from this chapter.

2.   Impact of the Asian financial crisis on China

The financial and economic crisis afflicting East Asia since mid 1997 has produced a major decline in GDP and industrial output growth across the region, as well as contributing to inflation in a number of countries due to the collapse of their currencies (see Table 10.1). These developments have impacted adversely on the Chinese economy in a number of ways, including: a decline in the country's export growth; a decline in its FDI; a deterioration in the corporate sector's profitability and most noticeably that of the SOEs; declining government revenue; increasing non-performing loans held by the state banks; rising unemployment from a combination of reform of the SOEs, downsizing of the government bureaucracy, and deteriorating external environment; and a further slowdown in China's GDP growth. From Table 10.2 the short-term outlook for the Chinese economy is for a noticeable decline in the economy's growth rate. Estimates for 1998 range from the more optimistic official figure of 8 per cent down to 6.7 per cent from a consensus of views by private forecasting agencies.[2] The State Statistical Bureau suggests that during 1998 the primary contribution to economic growth will be provided from fixed asset investment, mainly in the form of infrastructure expenditure, which forms the major component of the government's response to the deteriorating economic environment. The next major contribution will be provided from consumer retail sales and then exports (trade balance). Expectations are for a rise in consumer prices by 2.3 per cent during 1998, although this did not appear likely on the basis of developments by mid year. FDI is also anticipated to decline quite noticeably by about a third of its level in 1997 during 1998, due primarily to the financial crisis in the region.

While China's exports and FDI held up well during the initial stages of the regional crisis in 1997, they now appear to be more vulnerable as the extent of the regional crisis deepens beyond expectations. In addition, China's SOEs are being forced to reform in order to survive. In particular, emphasis is being placed upon raising their efficiency, cutting costs, rationalizing operations, and improving management. However, attempts to improve profitability have come at a social cost in the form of rapidly rising unemployment, the extent of which has already led to a rapidly deteriorating labour market. The deteriorating performance of the SOEs also has important implications for government revenue and the non-performing loans of the state banks. Together, all of these effects have contributed to a rapid deterioration in the economy's economic growth and labour market during 1998. As a consequence, policy has been focused upon reversing this situation as a matter of priority, and reform of the SOEs and banking sector has been slowed. However, most concern has focused upon external developments arising from the regional crisis.

Table 10.1 Internal economic developments – China and selected East
Asian economies, 1998

		(% Change on a Year Earlier)				
	GDP		*Industrial Production*		*Consumer Prices*	
China	+6.8	Q2 1998	+7.9	May 1998	−1.3	June 1998
Hong Kong	−2.8	Q1 1998	−4.0	Q1 1998	+4.0	June 1998
Taiwan	+5.9	Q1 1998	+5.4	June 1998	+0.9	July 1998
Malaysia	−1.8	Q1 1998	−8.6	May 1998	+6.2	June 1998
South Korea	−3.8	Q1 1998	−13.3	June 1998	+7.3	July 1998
Indonesia	−6.2	Q1 1998	+10.7	Q3 1997	+59.5	June 1998
Philippines	+1.7	Q1 1998	−7.7	Feb 1998	+10.6	July 1998
Singapore	+5.6	Q1 1998	−4.5	May 1998	−0.2	June 1998
Thailand	+0.4	1997	−17.5	May 1998	+10.0	July 1998

Source: *The Economist*, 8 August 1998, p. 88

About 85 per cent of foreign capital flowing into China comes from
Asia, equal to $US 38 billion out of a total of $US 45 billion in 1997.
However, the growth of FDI in China has been slowing more recently
for three major reasons. First, the main sources of FDI for China,
Hong Kong and overseas Chinese in Asian countries have suffered
severe setbacks arising from the financial and economic crisis in the
region. Second, foreign investment in Asia generally has contracted
due to the economic crisis afflicting the region. Finally, new FDI
commitments to China had already begun to slow down before the
crisis because of disappointment over returns on earlier investments,
a downward assessment of market potential in China, as well as
bureaucratic difficulties facing investors in China. FDI remained
strong during 1997 and during the first quarter of 1998. But over
the five months period from January to May 1998 it amounted to
$US 14.9 billion, some 1.5 per cent less than for the equivalent
period in 1997. Flows from a number of East Asian countries have
declined dramatically during the period of the crisis. For example,
Indonesian FDI in China is down 89.7 per cent, that by South Korea
is down by 55.8 per cent, that by Japan is down by 42.2 per cent and
that by Thailand is down by 35.5 per cent. However, there have been
increased inflows from Taiwan, Europe and the USA to offset this. FDI
by the EU is up by 75.4 per cent, and from the USA by 25.4 per cent.
Hence the early indications in 1998 are that declines in FDI by the

crisis-affected Asian economies in China, is being offset to some extent by that from the EU and USA in particular.

It is anticipated that there will be a likely fall in China's exports to crisis economies in East Asia. Net exports, or the trade balance, remained very strong after 1993, and exports contributed about 2 percentage points of China's total GDP growth of 8.8 per cent in 1997. However, its contribution was anticipated to weaken during 1998. During the first five months of 1998 exports increased by 7.6 per cent compared with a year previously, a sharp decline from the 20.9 per cent recorded for the whole of 1997. By May 1998 exports suffered their first year-on-year decline for 22 months, falling by 1.5 per cent. Some industries, such as textiles, are experiencing major difficulties. While China's trade has grown rapidly recently, its significance to the overall economy, however, should not be over-stated. Trade problems also threaten to hamper the reform programme. The government has been relying partly on the robust economic performance of its export-oriented coastal regions to provide employment for the millions of workers laid off due to SOE reform. Now that these areas are less able to take the strain, the pressures for delay in the government's industrial reforms have been further intensified.

Almost 30 per cent of China's exports in 1997 was to the economies of ASEAN, Korea and Japan, which have been badly affected by the financial and economic crisis. The ASEAN economies and Korea accounted for about 5 per cent each of China's total exports in 1997. Trade relations with Korea is complicated by the fact that many Korean export industries import components from China, and hence the net impact on trade is unclear. Although the growth of the Korean economy is slowing, any expansion by the export sector could lead to expanded demand for Chinese products, although this could be offset by the increased competition from the crisis economies due to their currency devaluations. For certain products such as clothes, cheap electronics and other light industry products China competes directly with a number of the ASEAN economies and especially Indonesia. However, to offset this Indonesian exporters are having considerable difficulty in gaining access to trade credit and to maintaining their credibility as reliable suppliers, and hence may be unable to take advantage of their improved competitiveness arising from their weaker exchange rate.

Table 10.2 Prospective developments in the Chinese economy during 1998

	Official	Development Bank	Private* Consensus	IMF	OECD**
1. – GDP Growth forecast (%)	8.0	7.2	6.7	7.0	7.1
2. Contributions to					
– GDP Growth***					
– Fixed Asset Investment	+14–15%	(Contribute 4–5 Percentage Points of GDP Growth)			
– Consumer Retail Sales	+8%	(Contribute 3–4 Percentage Points of GDP Growth)			
– Exports	+10%	(Net Trade up to 2 Percentage Points of GDP Growth)			
3. – Prices					
– CPI	+2.3%				
4. – FDI	$US 30 Billion	(–33.3% over 1997)			

*   Average prediction derived from EIU; Goldman Sachs; ING Barings; Merrill Lynch; J. P. Morgan; Salomon Smith Barney; Warburg Dillon Read

**   GNP growth

***   State Statistical Bureau, chief economist, Qiu Xiaohua comments

Source: Compiled from:
       China Government sources
       Asian Development Bank
       IMF
       OECD
       State Statistical Bureau
       The Economist

Japan accounted for about 17.5 per cent of China's exports in 1997, and hence the biggest external threat would come from a further slowdown in the Japanese economy. There is likely to be a moderate reduction in export growth to the USA and the EU (conservative fiscal and monetary policies in Europe because of the Euro, combined with the effects of greater competitiveness of ASEAN countries and Korea). The overall net effect is a likely export growth slowdown from about 21 per cent in 1997 to perhaps around 10 per cent in 1998. Sources in China[3] suggest that even with an export slowdown to 10 per cent in 1998 its impact upon the growth of the national economy would still be relatively moderate, but in some areas such as the coastal provinces, and cities such as Tianjin, the effect is likely to be felt more intensely.

In sum, such adverse external developments suggest it is unlikely that China can export its way out of its current slowdown predicament, and that more emphasis will need to be placed upon stimulating domestic demand. This indeed provides the basis for the government's policy response outlined in more detail in section 5 of this chapter.

3.   Will China devalue its currency?

Economic developments in the Chinese economy during 1998 and 1999 will have important regional and global implications. Should the downturn in the economy continue, and indeed intensify, it will contribute to a further increase in unemployment and rising social unrest, which will not only put in jeopardy the reforms in regard to the SOEs and banking system but could also result in intense pressure upon the authorities to devalue the currency. Hence if China's economic downturn deepens, the world, but more particularly the region, will be watching China's currency policy nervously. As the world's seventh largest economy, and its eleventh largest trading nation,[4] China's currency policy has immense regional and global repercussions. While many participants in the region's financial markets have suggested that the RMB needs to be devalued for the sake of Chinese competitiveness, a RMB devaluation would not be an appropriate response to the Asian crisis and is in fact unlikely. China has not been subject to the currency contagion affecting countries like Thailand, Indonesia, the Philippines

Table 10.3 External economic developments – China and Selected East asian economies, latest 12 months, 1998

	Trade Balance ($US Billion)		Current Account ($US Billion)		Foreign Exchange Reserves ($US Billion)		Exchange Rate Per $US		
							5 August '98	5 August '97	% Change
China	+45.0	June 1998	+24.6	1997*	140.9	June 1998	8.28	8.29	Neg
Hong Kong	−16.8	June 1998	−6.7	1997**	96.2	Apr 1998	7.75	7.74	Neg
Taiwan	+4.6	June 1998	+5.7	Q1 1998	84.4	May 1998	34.5	28.7	−20.2
Malaysia	+3.8	May 1998	−4.8	1997	21.3	Apr 1998	4.14	2.64	−56.8
South Korea	+24.7	July 1998	+23.4	June 1998	38.8	May 1998	1 265	894	−41.5
Indonesia	+17.7	May 1998	−5.8	Q4 1997	16.9	Apr 1998	12 900	2 585	−399.0
Philippines	−7.6	May 1998	−3.5	Q1 1998	7.8	Mar 1998	42.4	28.9	−46.7
Singapore	−0.5	June 1998	+13.6	Q1 1998	76.1	Apr 1998***	1.72	1.47	−17.0
Thailand	+4.8	May 1998	−2.9	Q1 1998	26.7	May 1998	40.9	31.0	−31.9

*   Estimate
**   Visible and Invisible Trade Balance
***   Includes Gold
Neg   Negligible
Source: *The Economist*, 8 August, 1998, p. 88.

and Korea due to: its successful macrostabilization measures since mid 1993; its strong agricultural performance over the past three years; and its strong external economic position. The RMB, it could be argued, is undervalued at current levels. A number of factors lie behind the relative strength of the currency, making the prospect of a devaluation unlikely. These include the following:

- **Strong external economic position** – China has experienced trade and current account surpluses since 1994, reaching record levels in 1997. In this year the country achieved a trade account surplus of $US 40 billion and a current account surplus of $US 24.6 billion. The most recent figures indicate that this situation still remains strong. Table 10.3 indicates that over the 12 month period to June 1998 the country attained a trade account surplus of $US 45 billion, and that this, as well as developments in the current account, compared very favourably with its regional neighbours. During the period January to June 1998 alone the trade surplus amounted to $US 18.6 billion, up by 33 per cent from a year earlier. Although export growth was slowing, import growth was declining even more.
- **China's export growth may not be adversely affected by devaluations elsewhere in East Asia** – Although devaluations elsewhere put Chinese exports in an unfavourable position, exchange rates are only one of many variables that affect export growth. For exchange rates to be significant in export competitiveness at least two conditions must be in place. First, products of competing nations must be so undifferentiated that they are nearly perfect substitutes for each other in world markets; and second, exports must embody the same proportions of capital, labour and technology as identical exports from competing economies. This is not the case in Asia, which consists of a number of diverse economies. The fall in the value of the Korean currency, for instance, may not have much impact on China's exports because Korean products tend to be more capital and technology intensive. However, devaluations in Indonesia, Malaysia, the Philippines and Thailand could have a larger impact on China. But China exports a more diverse range of products than these countries. Also, its labour costs are below the average for the region. Regional devaluations should reduce the

labour cost differential relative to China, but not eliminate it. In industries such as textiles and garments, where competition is intense, Southeast Asia is unlikely to take away significant market share from China, as such trade is mainly determined by non-tariff barriers imposed by leading importers such as the US. Direct competition with ASEAN countries is mainly limited to lower-end technology, electronics and sports articles – which overlap about 35 per cent of China's exports. For major exports, such as garments, toys, footwear, watches and clocks, China's sheer market share on global import markets offers a significant margin of protection. China's export tax (VAT export rebate below VAT import rate) has been reduced and is further reducible as an alternative to exchange rate adjustment so as to maintain exporters' competitiveness. Some industries are moving from coastal areas to the interior where labour and land costs are much lower. They do not relocate to Thailand and Indonesia. Even without moving to the interior, many of China's export industries remain competitive because of low production costs and the country's virtually unlimited pool of labour.

A Southeast Asian export surge seems unlikely in the near term. Many companies in the region are finding it difficult to import raw materials and parts and to obtain letters of credit and trade finance. In addition the overall disruption to their economic systems, including the high rates of bankruptcy, has increased costs of production and turned many firms into perceived unreliable suppliers, discouraging sales even though devaluations have made their prices more attractive.[5] Such difficulties do not face Chinese enterprises. This may be more important at present than a competitive exchange rate, and puts China's exporters at an advantage over their financially stricken regional competitors. The falling value of the yen also allows China to buy Japanese equipment more cheaply than before. There is also the prospect that if China can weather the economic storm in 1998 and the first half of 1999, domestic inflation in the crises countries will have greatly reduced their current competitive advantage.

Exports are, however, not the most important issue facing the country. Foreign trade still remains a relatively small part of overall economic activity,[6] important far more for the coastal provinces, which account for about a third of China's GDP, than the interior provinces. Although export growth appears to be slowing this is providing only a modest drag to the growth of the overall economy. Moreover, the RMB has become more competitive thanks to the sharp decline in inflation.

- **The currency is not fully convertible** – The currency is only fully convertible on current account, as of December 1996, but is not convertible on capital account and is therefore not subject to speculative attacks. As long as China maintains its sizeable surplus on the trade and current accounts, a weakening of the exchange rate will not occur. In fact there is evidence to suggest that upward pressure on the RMB remains, almost a year after the start of the Asian crisis. The government in early 1998 relaxed foreign exchange surrender requirements. Exporters have since accumulated $US 6 billion in foreign accounts, money that the Peoples' Bank of China would otherwise have had to buy to prevent an appreciation of the RMB. As indicated in Table 10.3, over the twelve-month period from 5 August 1997 – 5 August 1998, the exchange rate has remained very stable against the US dollar. This stands in sharp contrast to developments in the currencies of its regional neighbours, with the exception of Hong Kong due to its currency peg, which have experienced sizeable deteriorations during the period of the Asian financial crisis. Interestingly, the difference between the black market rate and the official rate for the RMB appears to be small, suggesting that the exchange rate is not much out of line with market sentiment. Arising from the Asian financial crisis the government has noted with concern the ability of a convertible currency to take a country's weak banking system to the point of collapse. The full convertibility of the currency is therefore likely to have been postponed indefinitely.
- **Substantial foreign exchange reserves** – China has very substantial foreign exchange reserves in absolute terms as well as relative to imports and short-term debt. Buoyant export growth and record capital inflows in 1997, particularly in the form of FDI, contributed to the accumulation of foreign exchange reserves worth $US 140 billion by the end of 1997. As indicated in Table 10.3 these stood at $US 140.9 billion by the end of June 1998[7] and compared very favourably with developments in other

regional economies. However, the growth of foreign reserves slowed down considerably during 1998. One reason is that since October 1997 exporters have been allowed to retain 15 per cent of their export earnings in US dollar assets, whereas previously all export earnings had to be sold on the foreign exchange market.

- **Limited exposure to foreign debt** – China's exposure to foreign debt is limited, amounting to only 17.3 per cent of GDP in 1997.[8] In addition, the bulk of its foreign debt stock is in long-term development loans and private FDI rather than in short-term debt.[9] As a percentage of total foreign exchange reserves, short-term debt amounted to only 27.6 per cent at end 1997, which compares very favourably with its regional neighbours.[10] In addition China, unlike its Asian neighbours, does not have a banking and financial system with substantial foreign debts denominated in overseas currencies. The country's bad debts in the banking system are denominated in RMB and not US dollars. Finally, China's two stock markets (excluding Hong Kong) are still relatively small and would not be capable of exerting a major impact on the economy arising from a change in market sentiment.

- **Strong domestic economy** – China has achieved a strong economic performance in comparison with that of other regional economies, and has attained much greater internal stability. As a result of the previously identified austerity measures implemented in China, the country has experienced a significant decline in its rate of inflation, and although a decline in GDP growth is anticipated in 1998, both by official and non-official sources, it still remains by far and away the highest in the region. The economy, unlike that of many of its neighbours, is less reliant for its growth on external developments. Total exports amounted to only 20 per cent of GDP in 1997. Chinese exports, in addition, are very import-intensive, except agricultural goods and processing industries such as cotton textiles and leather goods. Food exports account for about 10 per cent of China's total exports and textile exports are subject to MFA[11] quotas. Hence to try and stimulate the economy through a devaluation of the currency would not be particularly effective in comparison to policies aimed at stimulating domestic demand.

- **Negative implications for FDI of a devaluation** – If China were to devalue its currency, FDI would be hurt. Recent figures suggest that contracted FDI, new commitments by foreigners, has been declining, which is a major cause of concern to China's leaders. Foreign corporations committing capital in China to serve the local market, rely on a long-term strategy which assumes, among other things, a relatively stable exchange rate that more or less reflects market conditions. If the RMB were to be abruptly devalued, the dollar return on foreign investment in China would be reduced. This would also spark fears about future devaluations, and as such would not be a prudent policy at a time when investors are already jittery about emerging markets in general.

- **Devaluation and its impact on inflation** – Devaluation could also reignite the risk of inflation, which has abated on the back of tough austerity measures. Imports accounted for around 16 per cent of China's GDP in 1997. A devaluation would increase the domestic price of imports ranging from equipment to raw materials and intermediate goods, eventually leading to higher domestic prices for final consumption goods. Many of China's exports have a high import content, and hence this would offset any benefits from a devaluation. Sharply declining currencies elsewhere in Asia may not help reduce by much imported inflation for China, with the exception of a yen depreciation, as more than 85 per cent of its imports come from industrial economies and Hong Kong, whose currencies have not weakened in tandem with many of Asia's.

- **Adverse global and regional developments** – A devaluation could trigger off a host of adverse developments for the Chinese authorities. An abrupt change in China's exchange rate policy would destabilize the Hong Kong dollar peg to the US dollar, as well as its financial markets more generally, a consequence that China would prefer to avoid. Devaluation would cause friction with the US over an already spiralling bilateral trade imbalance in China's favour, which has allied diverse US groups, including labour unions, protectionist politicians, environmentalists and human rights activists, to lobby against China. Manipulating its exchange rate for trade advantages would also complicate China's negotiations on WTO membership. The WTO accession window is soon after US Congressional elections in the autumn. To enhance its WTO accession, China would be better to reduce its import restrictions and to protect its nominal exchange rate.

- **Maintaining regional stability** – As Asia's second largest economy, China's role in the region is critical in containing the financial crisis and stabilizing the regional economies. The government has been concerned by developments in the ASEAN 4[12] and South Korea, and its potential implications for China. While China has pledged financial support for Thailand and Indonesia[13] under IMF bailout packages, and forbore from objecting to Taiwanese contributions, the most effective assistance it can extend to its distressed neighbours is to maintain its own fast economic growth. A Chinese devaluation would likely trigger a fresh round of competitive devaluations in Asia, and aggravate the current regional economic crisis.[14] This would neither be to the region's benefit nor to China's. Hence, a currency devaluation would be an extremely risky strategy, in which the potential benefit to China's export competitiveness is, at best, uncertain, but the negative impact of such a policy could be severe. Hence, this strategy is one which China is unlikely to pursue as a response to the Asian financial crisis, and Premier Zhu Rongji has steadfastly refused to engage in a competitive devaluation. China's policy of developing constructive relations with ASEAN and other Asian neighbours, also makes devaluation unwanted for external political reasons.[15]

It is clear that China has a crucial role to play in what will now happen in Asia. Most analysts agree that a move by China to devalue its currency would set off a round of competitive devaluations and depression for the entire region, and the benefits to China from doing so are not at all clear.

4. China's regional economic leadership role

Because of a lack of determined leadership from Japan on the Asian economic and financial crisis, China has been thrust to centre stage. Indeed, at the recent Asia Europe meeting in London[16] Japan was heavily criticized for its lack of leadership in the economic recovery of Asia, and its lack of decisiveness over economic reform of its economy. Their prescriptions for Japan were tough, including: impose further tax cuts; boost domestic demand; and deregulate the economy. Otherwise it would not overcome its own economic slump, let alone that taking place in Asia. China, on the other hand, received considerable praise. For example, Leon Brittan (EU Trade Commissioner) praised China for 'her steady response to the Asian financial crisis, notably by resisting any devaluation of her currency ... and above all the startling pace of China's domestic reform agenda'. He also told a meeting of business leaders that 'no country in Asia – perhaps no country in the world – is more important for the future of the global economy than China'. Hence, the question must be asked as to whether the Asian financial crisis marks the start of a fundamental shift in economic leadership, with the world's most populous nation edging out the world's second largest economy as the regional engine of growth? Can, therefore, China play the role which the USA played in assisting the Latin American economies to overcome the 'tequila crisis' of 1994–95?

The reality is that China, at present, is in no position to fill the vacuum left by Japan. Plagued by its own internal economic problems, lack of resources and current level of development, China is far from becoming Asia's economic saviour. Rather than China playing the role of Asia's economic leader, Japan is simply not playing the role it should be playing. Even if China succeeds in getting its economic house in order (specifically SOE and banking sector reforms), it cannot in the foreseeable future provide the kind of economic leadership that Japan could (see Table 10.4). China simply does not have the resources – financial, technical or managerial – to lead Asia forward. Unlike China, Japan, for instance, has enormous multinational companies to invest capital and transfer technology. Japan's investment and official development assistance

Table 10.4   Economic significance of Japan and China, 1996 *($US billion)*

	China	Japan
GDP	827	4 599.7
Imports (cif)	131.5	349.3
Overseas Direct Investment	2.1	23.4
Overseas Portfolio Investment	0.6	114.6
Official Development Assistance	n/a	11.1

Source: International Monetary Fund, *International Financial Statistics*, April, 1998
China Statistical Yearbook, 1997 Overseas Economic Cooperation Fund (Japan)

is considerably larger than that of China's. Ultimately, no matter how inward looking or troubled Japan becomes, it will remain Asia's economic leader for the foreseeable future. China may one day be ready to take over the economic mantle, but that could be up to 10–15 years away, if not more.

While China can make an important contribution to developments in the Asian and global economies, particularly through its commitment to not devaluing the RMB and its attempts to prevent a further slowdown in its economy, some economist believe that the country actually poses a threat to the stability and economic recovery of the region in particular, and the global economy in general. The reasons for this are as follows:

- **China's weak banking system** – with official estimates putting non-performing loans at 20 per cent of the total, considerable restructuring/reform of the financial/banking system will be required before these banks can be put on a commercial footing. If this is not done it could cause major problems to the economy in the future and consequently the region, as has happened for a number of other countries,
- **China's stockpiles of inexpensive consumer goods** – these have arisen from the boom years of 1992–95 and the over-capacity in many industries which has resulted. This could represent a major threat to the exports of countries like Thailand, Indonesia and the Philippines, and make a recovery of their economies more difficult,
- **China is a major and successful exporter** – its current and advantageous position relative to its regional neighbours will enable it to consolidate its strong market position, making it more difficult for the Asian crisis economies to compete,
- **China attracts major inflows of FDI** – the country attracts major inflows of FDI, because of its relative attractiveness, which its neighbours desperately require to assist their economic recovery,
- **China has the most abundant and cheapest labour in Asia** – which enables it to maintain its competitiveness despite its less competitive exchange rate, again making it difficult for its neighbours to compete,
- **China will not take many exports from its neighbours** – China's imports, including machinery, technology and wheat, comes mostly from the US, Japan and Europe. Hence, the preven-

tion of a further downturn in its economy will not have a major influence on the exports of its regional neighbours.

5.   Policy response to the economic slowdown

Since March 1998, the Chinese authorities have been implementing a domestic stimulus package, described as a Chinese style 'New Deal', in response to the economy's deteriorating domestic and external circumstances, that will increase expenditure on public works and other projects by as much as 20 per cent per year. Emphasis will be placed on infrastructure investment and on housing construction. By focusing upon internal growth, the Chinese are signalling their resolve not to out-export their neighbours, and to maintain their pledge of not devaluing the RMB. The key components of this new deal, in detail, are as follows:

- **Increased infrastructure development**: In February 1998 in Davos Switzerland, at the World Economic Summit, Chinese Vice Premier Li Lanqing announced a $US 750 billion infrastructure and environment plan for China (to be spread over three years), the aim of which being to keep economic growth in China above 8 per cent in 1998. This gave the clearest indication that the Chinese authorities were concerned about, and saw the need to respond to, the slowing economy. Such an increase in infrastructure expenditure and fixed-asset investment could boost GDP by an estimated extra 2 per cent. While the country certainly needs better roads, airports, railways, ports, bridges and irrigation schemes, housing, posts and telecommunications, particularly in the poorer inland provinces, the issue of how the programme was to be funded, without fuelling inflation, needed to be resolved. The government is already running budget deficits, and this programme, in conjunction with declining SOE revenue, will substantially increase the 1998 state budget deficit to as much as $US 5.5 billion according to some estimates. However, with a budget deficit of just 0.7 per cent of GDP in 1997 and low domestic debt, China can afford to finance more new infrastructure projects with the issue of government bonds.

  A number of funding options exist. Much of it is anticipated to come from the country's vast personal savings, some $US 560 billion accumulated during the period of economic reform and held as deposits at the state-run commercial banks throughout the country, and by expanding directed lending by the state banks. Domestic savings could be mobilized in a variety of ways: through the sale of central government bonds; letting cities and provincial governments sell bonds both locally and internationally for local projects; expanding the sale of corporate bonds which are restricted at present to under $US 2 billion a year; and increasing the number of highway and railroad bonds. The government could attempt to raise funds in the Hong Kong financial markets, but the market is currently depressed and there are few relatively good investment projects. Another option is to expand, and tap into, existing 'extra-budgetary' revenue. Attracting foreign investors on a build, operate and transfer basis (BOT) is possible but would be difficult for projects in the poorer inland provinces. Utilizing these alternatives means some 117 key infrastructure projects are to be carried out this year, more single projects than in any previous year.

- **Mass residential housing programme**: The second major component of the programme is the construction of low-cost housing with the objective of encouraging home ownership. The potential of this component of the programme is substantial, but is unlikely to have an immediate impact. Many residential developments already stand vacant, and convincing Chinese people to buy rather than to rent will take time. State subsidized rents would need to go much higher before consumers would consider buying their own homes. Under proposed government reforms, as of 1 July 1998, state housing was only to be made available for sale and not rent, and rent for existing tenants was to be increased to 15 per cent of family income or to the market level. Such developments, it was anticipated, would expand the nascent consumer finance industry, stimulate specifically a housing mortgage market, as well as other services industries such as insurance and underwriting and other property ownership infrastructure. It would take time, however, for a country with an undeveloped financial system. In addition, the development of a private housing market, including the sale of the current stock of housing to its occupants, would enhance labour mobility and enable the development of an effective labour market. As long as housing is limited and largely controlled by existing enterprises, labour mobility will be limited and new enterprise creation inhibited. This is particularly the case for smaller enterprises that do not have the capacity to provide housing for their employees. Private housing would also encourage the creation of small enterprises not only in construction, but also in maintenance and home improvement, including plumbers, carpenters, painters and electricians. New housing units would in turn give rise to demands for new consumer products, such as appliances and furniture. Such a housing programme, therefore, has the potential to be an important engine for growth. However, as the economy, and in particular the labour market, has steadily deteriorated during 1998, the government postponed reform of state housing until the end of 1998, being concerned that rising rents and sale of the existing stock of housing would reduce funds available for consumption expenditure and thereby exacerbate the economic slowdown.

- **Monetary measures:** As part of the new deal programme, the central bank has eased the austerity measures in place since 1993 in two major ways. First, pressure has been brought to bear on the state banks to expand access to credit for key sectors such as that of infrastructure, exporters, and for home purchase consistent with attaining the overall objectives of the programme, as well as to struggling SOEs. Consistent with this, interest rates have been reduced to further stimulate infrastructure investment and house purchase. At the end of June 1998 the monetary authorities announced the fifth interest rate cut in just over a year, with commercial bank lending rates cut by an average of 1.12 percentage points to 6.5 per cent for loans up to six months and around 6.9 per cent for loans up to one year. Monetary policy alone, however, has major limitations in the present climate of excess capacity and depressed domestic demand, and its current role is therefore primarily to facilitate the attainment of the other major components of the programme in stimulating aggregate expenditure.

- **Maintain the reform momentum:** While the first three components can contribute to alleviating the short-term downturn in the economy, additional measures will be required to ensure that the growth momentum is maintained over the medium to long term. This will involve: pushing ahead with reform of the SOEs; reforming the banking sector; restructuring the economy; and reducing the size of government. As indicated in an earlier section, major developments are under way in these areas. However, the rapid deterioration of the economy has contributed to a rapid increase in unemployment and rising concern over social unrest. This has already led to an effective reversal of banking sector reform, with state banks once again being required to extend easy loans to key sectors of the economy. Further reform of the SOEs also appears to be slowing down.

- **Tax rebates for exporters:** The government has offered exporters special tax rebates on exports of coal, textiles, rolled steel, cement and some machinery products to offset the loss of competitiveness brought about by the relatively strong RMB.

In addition to these core components of the stimulatory package, additional measures, or added dimensions, are likely to be required in order to make it successful:

- **Open up the interior provinces of China:** Opening up the interior provinces has the potential to boost domestic demand significantly. The government must attempt to ensure that its ambitious public works programme will spread the wealth to such interior cities as Wuhan and Zhengzhou. In addition it is also important to assist the three-quarters of China's population that lives in rural areas, but which accounts for only 45 per cent of retail sales. This is clearly a longer-term strategy but with considerable potential for maintaining the growth momentum. There will need to be an important role for foreign investors in this process, who should be encouraged to invest in the interior where costs are lower rather than in coastal provinces. The establishment of appropriate infrastructure and other incentives would greatly assist in this process.
- **Create incentives to attract more FDI:** One of the ways to generate further employment growth is to continue attracting FDI. Contracted FDI has declined significantly recently, suggesting that there is a need to accelerate the approval rate for new private and joint venture projects, and establish a more investor friendly environment.

- **Improve the social security system and worker retraining**: With the prospect over the short to medium term of further substantial increases in urban unemployment and rising social unrest, it will be essential to put a more substantive safety net in place for displaced workers. In addition, there will be a need to retrain such workers for new employment opportunities in the rapidly expanding services sector, or for the prospective establishment of their own small businesses.
- **Devalue the RMB:** Should the government be unable to revive economic growth through the new deal programme, and if rising unemployment and social unrest are creating major instability, in conjunction with pressure from business interests such as that of shipbuilding, petrochemicals and steel, the authorities may become sufficiently desperate to devalue the currency. If conducted, it should be done so only gradually to avoid a major disturbance. However, this would be a last-resort policy, and if utilized would clearly indicate that the authorities had lost control of macroeconomic developments elsewhere.

Many of these measures have the major drawback that they will only have a lagged effect upon the economy. While the speeding up of infrastructure projects should have a relatively quick impact upon output and employment, and hence has received most emphasis, the authorities should not neglect the other measures, so as to ensure the longer-term health of the economy. Otherwise the same situation may have to be faced up to again, but be more intractable next time around.

6.   Summary and conclusions

China is currently facing a downturn in the rate of growth of its economy. During the period of economic reform, since 1978, such an economic downturn has not been uncommon, having generally occurred after the authorities implemented measures to curb bouts of inflationary pressure. The current downturn is quite different from that experienced in the past, in that the economy is experiencing excess supply relative to demand, exemplified by: over-capacity in many industries; high stock levels; price deflation; declining retail sales growth; and declining growth of fixed-asset investment. On top of this, the Asian financial crisis is bringing about declining export growth and inflows of FDI. Lacklustre demand is seen as being the primary culprit, rather than tight credit, and therefore traditional methods of kick starting the economy, easing credit and expanding fixed-asset investment, will not work this time. A new approach will be required.

To this end the government has put in place a 'new deal' programme emphasizing: a public works programme focusing upon infrastructure spending; housing reform; a further loosening of monetary policy; but no devaluation of the currency to boost exports. There are tremendous risks involved if this programme of measures is unsuccessful in reversing, over the short term, the downward growth trend of the economy. As the economic environment continued to deteriorate during 1998, expediency has required the authorities to focus policy on the need to reverse this downward trend in the short term, and to place less emphasis on reforms required for the medium- to long-term health of the economy. Growth of less than 7–8 per cent will not be enough to absorb a growing army of laid off workers and new labour market entrants. Social unrest would loom large. The recent experience of Indonesia would pale into insignificance if the equivalent occurred in China, which would be hugely damaging for the regional and global economies.

Notes

1. In April 1998 Huang Yukon, chief representative of the World Bank in Beijing, argued that growth below 5 per cent would initiate substantial unrest.
2. This contrasts with an average annual GDP growth rate of 11.6 per cent over the period 1992–97.
3. State Statistical Bureau chief economist.
4. See IMF, *International Financial Statistics*, March 1998.
5. See, for example, Stiglitz (1998).
6. The trade balance in 1997 was equivalent to about 4.4 per cent of GDP, in 1996 the figure was 1.5 per cent of GDP.
7. These reserves were second only in the world to that of Japan's, which stood at $US 219.6 billion at end 1997.
8. As at December 1997. This compares with the equivalent figures for Indonesia – 62.4 per cent, Korea–32 per cent, Malaysia – 43.3 per cent, Philippines – 62.3 per cent, Taiwan – 15.2 per cent, and Thailand – 62.9 per cent. These figures were obtained from J.P. Morgan.

9. Short-term debt comprised only 24.9 per cent of total foreign debt, or 4.3 per cent of GDP at end 1997. The equivalent figures for Indonesia are 27.2 per cent and 17 per cent, for Korea 37.3 per cent and 11.9 per cent, for Malaysia 29.8 per cent and 12.9 per cent, for the Philippines 24.7 per cent and 15.4 per cent, for Taiwan 67.9 per cent and 10.3 per cent, and for Thailand 29.2 per cent and 18.4 per cent respectively.
10. The equivalent figure, at end 1997, for Indonesia is 184 per cent, for Korea is 250 per cent, for Malaysia is 59.4 per cent, for the Philippines is 172 per cent, for Taiwan is 36 per cent, and for Thailand is 108 per cent.
11. Multi Fibre Agreement.
12. Indonesia, Malaysia, Philippines and Thailand.
13. $US 1 billion in each case.
14. A point fully elaborated upon by Liu Lanqing, Vice Premier, at the World Economic Forum, Davos, Switzerland, February 1998.
15. The promise not to devalue the RMB was again reiterated in early June 1998 by central bank governor Dai Xianglong at a time when the Japanese currency came under further downward pressure.
16. May 1998.

References

Asiaweek, various, Asiaweek Limited, Hong Kong.

Bottelier, P. (1998), China's prospects in light of the Asian crisis, presentation at the SAIS China Forum, Johns Hopkins University, USA, March.

Businessweek (1998), Can China avert a crisis?, McGraw-Hill Inc., March 16.

Department of Foreign Affairs and Trade (1997), *China embraces the market*, East Asian Analytical Unit, Canberra.

Far Eastern Economic Review, various, Review Publishing Company Limited, Hong Kong.

Financial Times (1998), China: alarm bells hasten reforms, Financial Times Newspaper Limited, April 27.

Financial Times (1998), China: engines start going into reverse, Financial Times Newspaper Limited, May 20.

Harvie, C. (1997), 'Reforming China's state owned enterprises: what can be learned from the experiences of other economies in transition', University of Wollongong, Department of Economics, Working Paper Series, WP 97–1.

IMF (1997), *World Financial Outlook – Interim Assessment*, Washington, DC, December.

IMF (1998), *World Economic Outlook*, Washington, DC, May.

Stiglitz, J. (1998), Second-generation strategies for reform for China, Address given at Beijing University, Beijing, China, 20 July.

The Economist, various, The Economist Newspaper Limited, London, UK.

The South China Morning Post (1998), 'Demand slowdown pressures central bank on cuts', South China Morning Post Publishers Ltd, Hong Kong.

Washington Post, (1998), 'China's economic ills may imperil region', The Washington Post Company, February 11.

Washington Post (1998), 'China announces large bond issue to bail out banks', The Washington Post Company, March 1.

Washington Post (1998), 'Zhu vows to boost China's economy', The Washington Post Company, March 20.

Washington Post (1998), 'Analysts seek new deal, China style', The Washington Post Company, April 25.

11
Where Do We Go From Here?

Tran Van Hoa

In the preceding chapters, international experts in the areas have provided us with valuable studies on the Asian economic and financial crisis, their cures as diagnosed and advocated for adoption by national and international agencies, and the debates on their effectiveness in the countries in trouble. While the search for the real causes of the crisis has achieved some consensus – that is, the consensus that foreign trade and its international competitiveness have been empirically and analytically the driving force for growth and development in many Asian economies, including some advanced countries in the region, such as Singapore and Japan, in the past few decades. It is this very foreign trade and the slowdown of it in an environment of economic globalization and electronic commerce and finance, that has contributed significantly to the Asian turmoil and its damaging contagion worldwide.

The general assessment is that the cures and remedies, as prescribed by the International Monetary Fund and adopted by many Asian economies after numerous tenuous negotiations, have been ineffective in arresting the Asian meltdown and in restarting growth and development in the region. Worse still, the impact of the crisis has been observed in countries as far away from the region as Russia, Argentina, Brazil, the USA and Germany. Many efforts by major countries (e.g. the USA) or groups of countries (e.g. the OECD and APEC) in the world have failed for a number of reasons to gather enough consensus and to produce practical solutions (e.g. the lowering of interest rates worldwide) to solve the crisis and its contagion.

In this scenario, the prospects from our analyses in the preceding chapters appear to be less than promising for Asian and world economies, at least in the next few years. This general conclusion should have its proper perspective: that is, it helps to set a focus on further efforts by the international community to collectively and simultaneously formulate and implement feasible and operational plans to promote growth, development and trade in domestic and international economies.

12
Postscript: Prospects in Asia Update

Tran Van Hoa

1. Overview

This book contains details of recent surveys and analyses dealing with the fundamental aspects for a number of major countries affected by the Asia crisis, evaluating the various rescue packages and reforms, and also exploring the prospects for them in both the short and the long term. The prognosis of our contributing authors has been that the prospects for growth, development, trade, investment, business and welfare improvement for these countries are not as good as predicted by national and international policy-makers at least for the near or medium-term future.

Two main factors can be seen as producing this kind of assessment. First, the fundamental cause of the Asia crisis seems to be a slowdown in foreign trade in a number of countries in the region, and these issues have not been improved in spite of the various rescue packages adopted by international organizations (e.g. the International Monetary Fund and the World Bank) and national economic and political reforms. Second, while most Asian economies have enjoyed strong competitiveness in productivity and growth, their competitiveness in finance and banking has been far below the international average. This state of the financial and banking sector and the size of corporate debts in most economies in Asia have not been rectified despite vigorous national and international debates on the issues.

The problem is perhaps compounded by the fact that the international economy is entering a cyclical downturn towards the millennium.

It should be noted, however, that, as of June 1999, there are some signs of economic recovery in Asia: 1.9 and 4.6 per cent growths posted by Japan and South Korea respectively in the first quarter of 1999. However, many experts and policy-makers (e.g. US Treasury Secretary Rubin) have agreed that one or two figures do not tell whether the situation is good or bad. In addition, a serious analysis of the trends of major economic and financial aggregates in many Asian countries does not auger well for better prospects.

2.   An update

In April 1999 China's leaders issued, at the National People's Congress, the tough warning that the external economic environment faced by China is still grim as financial discipline is lax and the economic order is in disarray. As economic growth continues to show serious signs of downturn, the Chinese government has decided to fall back to the 1930s' economic prescription of increased fiscal spending (with a 57 per cent increase in the budget deficit) to maintain the levels of expansion to check the increased risk of social instability caused by rising unemployment. There is also talk of further devaluation of the Chinese currency with its potential adverse effects on the deepening crisis worldwide. China's central bank has responded to a slowing-down economy by slashing interest rates for the seventh time in less than four years.

Indonesia is remodelling its political system and, on 7 June 1999, held its election to effect a transition to democracy. The Indonesian government and most analysts are not predicting a disintegration of the country, but they have assumed that the price of failure in the process will be very high, not just for Indonesia but for the entire region, too. In this climate of change and uncertainty the prospects for economic recovery after a profound economic crisis and a breakdown in law and order in many parts of the country do not seem promising. In fact, international analysts have predicted that the uncertain political outlook and social tensions may add to the risks, implying that economic stability may not return to Indonesia for some years.

In Thailand the quick economic recovery has failed to occur and future improvement in growth and development is also uncertain. Undoubtedly an influence here was the 'normal' Thai political standard, which again asserted itself in 1999, putting at risk the hard-won reforms of the recent past and the quality of the country's eventual recovery.

The economy of Japan shrank 0.8 per cent in the December quarter of 1998, making an annual contraction of 3.2 per cent and a record 15 months of recession. While government policy, which is based essentially on the Great Depression ideas, seems to be heading in the right direction, the recovery is weak, with restructuring, unemployment, less capital spending, falling wages, weak demand and less revenue for small and medium-size businesses. The government has almost run out of revival policies, with interest rates already near zero and public debt above 100 per cent of GDP.

The political and economic outlook for Malaysia has brightened after a year of crisis that sent the economy into a nose-dive and generated fears of widespread unrest. Indonesia-style social turmoil has not happened in Malaysia. The financial gloom, predicted by many analysts after Malaysia turned away from IMF proposals for economic recovery, has not occurred. On the contrary, the easing of credit and interest rates and the imposing of capital controls have stabilized the currency and stock markets and brought a degree of relief to the business community. Exporters have continued to find markets, while imports have declined, giving rise to a favourable balance of trade and a boost in central bank reserves by about $US7 billion. With a forecast growth of 1–3 per cent for 1999, following last year's contraction of 6.7 per cent, foreign fund managers have found Malaysia a more optimistic economy and a relatively good place to invest. It has been argued by many analysts that other fundamental problems still persist in Malaysia. These include its industrial infrastructure, a shortage of engineers, managers and other senior personnel. In addition, analysts have predicted that the current account surplus under the 'crisis' situation is not sustainable over the long run.

3.   Prospects in other Asian economies

The prospects for those Asian economies not covered in this book are also not that promising. Singapore, which is poised between mild recession and modest growth in 1999, is facing another uncertain year. Hong Kong remains hostage to a sluggish world economy and especially to the deflationary process that besets the mainland. Taiwan's prospects for economic growth remain modest in 1999, especially since the eruption of a domestic financial crisis in late 1998, and early 1999 promises to drag down private investment and consumption, with the slowest expansion since 1983 (4.74 per cent predicted for 1999). Myanmar, isolated by its isolationist policy and human rights shortfalls, faces stagnating foreign direct investment due to the country's introduction of severe import controls to shore up the failing economy. The Philippines, with its large workforce overseas, remitting $US10 billion a year in foreign exchange reserves to the country, seems to have avoided the worst impact of the Asia crisis. But it posted only a 0.1 per cent growth in 1998. The Greater Mekong subregion (Vietnam, Cambodia, Laos, Myanmar and southern China), which was actively supported as a major project for detailed study and development by the Asian Development Bank in the early 1990, is now drifting in the Asian meltdown.

Index